PETE CUNNINGHAM

GOD'S MESSENGER BOY

A STORY OF FAITH IN ACTION FOR THE HOMELESS

TORCH RUNNER
PUBLICATIONS

Contents

Endorsement

"I have known Pastor Pete for many years, and he remains an inspiration to me. Inspired by deep humility and service to the Lord, he has developed an enterprising model to tackle homelessness and rebuild lives and I would commend the Green Pastures story to everyone."

Andrew Selous MP
Second Church Estates Commissioner

Dedication

I really would like to thank every Christian I have ever come into contact with in my life, for I am persuaded that they all have played a part in making me the person I am today. So, let me just name a few.

- My brother, Paul, whose persistence in talking to me about Christ brought me to a knowledge of the Lord Jesus.

- The persistence of my pastor, Norman Young, who never gave up on me.

- Keith Monument, who allowed me to do two years as a herald.

- Ray Belfield, who took me under his wing for ministry.

- The congregation at Bramley who put up with the hectic ride for four years.

- The three young men who came and worked alongside me: Norman, Danny, and Dennis.

- The oversight of Bishop Auckland Church who helped me see Christianity in a fresh light.

- Miss Cloak, who took me on to run the church in Southport in the early nineties together with hundreds more.

- Finally, to my wife who has put up with me, to my sons Andrew and Simon who have worked alongside me in the last twenty years, and Vic Woodley, a constant companion in times of trouble.

All these have brought us to the place we are today. A huge thanks to everyone.

Foreword

This book glows with the joy of Pete's journey with God. It's a story of courage and perseverance told with great warmth and empathy. Themes of building, sharing, and faith recur throughout the pages, which are brought to life with Pete's endearing style.

There are moments of great insight and humour as Pete's recalls his early working life in the City in the '60s, where he found himself an unwitting messenger for God. His faith shines through every page as he finds God-sent encouragement in the most unlikely of places, including the passengers of a train bound for the north of England.

As the story unfolds, we see the seed of an idea blossom into Green Pastures, a ministry which helps house the homeless, founded by Pete. It's a journey of struggle, but ultimately triumph, a marathon not a sprint, with God clearly directing the pace and direction of travel.

Filled with hope and encouragement, it's a rallying cry to listen to God and step out in faith with a warm heart and a ready smile. You never know what might happen! Pastor Pete certainly didn't but trusted in the Lord every step of the way!

Amanda Bindon
Chief Executive
www.cinnamonnetwork.co.uk

Part I

GOD'S MESSENGER BOY

Chapter 1

There was a shattering sound of glass as a beautiful eight-day travel clock met the floor, disintegrating into a thousand pieces. I had lost my temper again with my brother Paul. He seemed to insist on talking to me about Jesus. I hated it and was determined to have nothing to do with religion or church or Christianity.

I was 18 years old and living the high life. Ever since my father was tried at the Old Bailey when I was 10 years old, my family had become religious maniacs in my eyes. My father, a habitual gambler at the time, had stolen money from his firm to feed his habit and was duly sent to the Old Bailey for trial. While he was in the cells below awaiting sentence, a man came and spoke to him about Jesus Christ. The words of this preacher touched my father's heart and changed him forever as he accepted Christ into his life. Afterward a strange program of change entered the family, and I found myself attending a London City Mission where the local preacher, the Reverend Pearcy, preached hellfire every Sunday evening. My mother, my sister, and my brother Paul all became ardent Christians, and so began eleven years of what I thought was purgatory.

At the age of fifteen, to escape the insanity of my family, I left home with a friend and became a beach bum down in New Quay. For nearly three months, I lived by scrounging around and living off the good nature of people. If I say so myself, I was quite a handsome and engaging young man, which meant that I related well to old and young, male and female, with a beguiling and entertaining nature bringing me friendships on a continual basis. Then one night, I was picked up by the police for a minor crime, put into the cells for a night, and then ignominiously put on a train and sent home to my parents.

For the next two months, I spent my life in bed. My mother, who I now know was a wonderful woman, would not allow me to become a layabout and wrote for interviews for me to attend. It was this that landed me a job in stockbroking in the London Stock Exchange. I was originally employed at sixteen as a Messenger Boy, which involved delivering transfer documents of stocks or shares. I progressed from there to becoming what was known as a Red Button, which permitted me to enter the Stock Exchange in the office below the floor of the house. In those days, a broker would purchase or sell shares on behalf of their clients to what was commonly known as a Jobber. The Jobber dealt in certain companies, and you could either buy or sell stocks of that company to that Jobber. The work of the Red Button was to enter the Stock Exchange with a list of transactions that his broker had completed the day before and check that the amount of stock that was sold as well as the price agreed was correct. I found all this fascinating as I would see sometimes millions of pounds transacted in one deal, particularly in Treasury Stocks often called Gilt Switches. Then to my joy, I was promoted to working on the floor of the house, which allowed me to get prices from Jobbers for my broker's clients.

Math had always been my favourite subject, and by the time I was eighteen, I was one of the youngest unauthorized clerks on the floor of the house of the Stock Exchange. How God leads us in these areas of "training" amazes me even today, for understanding financial markets and buying and selling certainly has helped me in our Ministry of Green Pastures, which is so successful today. Working at the Stock Exchange, my wages were excellent, my bonuses were phenomenal, and I lived a life of Riley. By the time I became a Christian, I had a dozen suits in my wardrobe, was going out with three women, and mixing with some of the nobles of our land.

It was in November of 1963 that I attended the Goldsmiths Art Academy Ball. This is the top art academy in London, renowned throughout the world. I had made friends with a number of the students there, and they had invited me. That night, I was bored out of my trolley, and so I mixed the drinks I had that evening, from Dubonnet to Rum Chasers to Courvoisier—which is an excellent Brandy —and finally found myself in the live art studio collapsed in a heap on a pile of hay, paralytically drunk. My legs felt like lead, and I could not move. My friends found me at 2 a.m., and by then, they were pretty drunk too. They grabbed me by the arms and lifted me into an upright position, put my arms around their shoulders, carried me out of the building, and bundled me into their car.

The journey was just a haze to me. They took me back to their flat where I stayed Saturday and Sunday. Only after I had finished work on Monday did I return home. My family, who had not known my whereabouts over the weekend, were extremely agitated as I had not let them know what was going on. Eventually, an almighty row developed between myself and my father. His temper matched mine, and we nearly came to blows. My father concluded that he could no longer put up with me living in our family home and the only way forward was for me to move out of the house that evening.

The reason I was living at home was that, although I was supposed to pay rent, I never paid any. My mother kept a notebook which added up the arrears that I owed. I was something in the region of £400 in arrears, which in the equivalent money today would be £4,000. So, in some ways, I was not concerned. In fact, I couldn't care a raspberry. I had a very pleasing personality and perhaps a charming way, which is why I had lots of friends on the Stock Exchange and outside in the nighttime community. And so, I knew at least four flats I could go and live in.

As I carried my suitcase down the stairs ready to exit the family home with no regrets and looking forward to my future adventures, my path was blocked by my beautiful mother, who loved me dearly and longed for me to come to know Christ. She was in a heated discussion with my father about my future.

I remember the words of my mother as she pleaded my case. "Harold, what will become of him if we let him leave?" My father heeded to her pleas and said that I could stay, but I would need to obey some rules that he would put into place, and I was no longer to come into the house drunk, which I had frequently done. In fact, I would say, at least twice a week, being very tipsy was a common occurrence. I was also not to bring any women there, which was again a common habit I was into.

That night when my brother arrived home, he understood that there had been ructions in the house and that expulsion from the family home was now on the cards for his younger brother. Paul never missed the opportunity of trying to win me, his wayward brother, to Christ. So the next morning, while we were getting dressed, he began to talk to me again about church. In a very pleasing voice, he said to me, "Pete, why don't you come to church this Saturday? We have a special youth rally on. You might find it interesting."

I considered the fact that, as I had lined up six or seven Christmas parties to go to, it might be good for me to attend church as a ruse to my parents who might even consider that I was about to make a change in my life's direction. So, I agreed to go.

When I arrived at the church in Canning Town, the place began to fill with young men and women. They sang lustily the choruses of the day and the place rocked with music. Then they invited a man called Donald Gee to get up and speak to the young people who had assembled.

While I was sitting at the back of the church, looking at the gentleman who had risen to his feet with his ancient dress, I inwardly laughed my socks off since I could not contain my mocking view of him. This man was seventy-five if he was a day; he was portly, with a suit that had a waistcoat and, believe it or not, a pocket watch and chain dangling from it. A bald patch down the centre of his head with two areas of grey hair on either side, he had pince-nez eyeglasses and jowls that hung from his chin to his chest. How could this elderly gentleman, who appeared to have one foot in the grave, appeal to young men and women?

He preached for about twenty minutes, and as he came to the end of his speech, he said one thing that lodged in my mind. "Young man, young woman, if you have never given God an opportunity in your life, how can you say it does not work?"

Most nights over the next six weeks, that question haunted me. Some evenings, when I would return from a party partially drunk, I would lay on my bed, the room would slowly spin, and the words would come back to me. *You have never given God an opportunity in your life, how can you say it doesn't work?*

Chapter 2

When salvation came, it was swift, sudden, and certainly unexpected. After attending the youth meeting my brother had invited me to, my parents took the pressure off, and I was able to go to all the parties that I had lined up for December and January. I met two wonderful young women. The first woman, Bunty, came to work in our office at the Stock Exchange. She was the daughter of one of the partners, who was the third son of an earl. Wow, what a conquest! I was going out with a girl who was the daughter of a landed gentry, and my, she was hot! Two of the parties I attended during that Christmas season were in the homes of well-heeled families. I began to feel that I had really arrived on the society scene.

The second woman was named Linda. After going out with a number of my male friends one evening and all of us becoming a little merry, someone told us of a party that was going on just attended by women. We piled into our cars, drove to the house, knocked on the door and entered without invitation. It was the sixteenth birthday party of the girl who lived there. Her parents had gone out. What a place for hungry young men looking for love and romance. Linda was sitting in a corner, pretty and dark haired. I made my way across to her, and she smiled nicely. I noticed that she had two dimples in her cheeks, one on either side. So, my chat up line was, "Hello, your name must be Debbie Dimples," to which she shyly replied, "No, it is Linda." Then the parents of the girl arrived. To say the least, they were not pleased to see a group of very merry young men mixing with their daughter and her friends, and so they began to evict us. I offered Linda a ride home in the car, and in due course, deposited her outside her home on Selwyn Avenue with an arrangement for her to call me at a later date.

So, the round of social events went well, finishing with one of the best New Year's Eve parties in my life. Having arrived home at two o'clock in the morning on January 1, 1964, I slept soundly until 7:30 a.m. After awakening, I just could not get back to sleep, so around 8 a.m., I arose, washed, and dressed, and prepared a hearty breakfast. I began pondering, "What shall I do with the day?" Suddenly, a crazy thought filtered into my mind. "It is January the first. Let's make some New Year's resolutions. Let's try to do something good, helpful, innovative, world-changing. Let us turn over a new leaf and become a better person." I then realised it was a Sunday, and my brother's church would be open. What if I went to church? That would be different. So, with that resolve in mind, I decided that going to church would be a good start.

At 9:30 a.m., I set out to walk to my brother's church. As far as I was aware, the service started at 10:30 a.m., and I arrived just in time. However, that was the time people gathered to pray and the real service didn't begin till 11 a.m. So I entered the church, crossed over to the left-hand side, and on the fourth row from the front, I moved in and sat against the wall. The church began to fill, and there were now five of us sitting in that row.

When the service began, the congregation began to zealously sing a hymn. "Would you be free from your burden of sin? There's power in the blood, power in the blood; Would you live daily a victory to win? There is wonderful power in the blood." Then they sang the chorus with even greater gusto, "There is power, power, wonder-working power, In the blood of the Lamb; There is power, power, wonder-working power, In the precious blood of the Lamb." I felt like a fish out of water. What was I doing there? Had I lost my mind? I was sitting amongst a group of religious fanatics, but the problem was I couldn't get out. I was blocked in by the other four people sitting in the row. I felt embarrassed to leave and push past them, so I thought in my head, "If ever I get out of this place today, I will never return to church." Little did I understand what the gracious Almighty had planned for me on that wonderful day.

The congregation sat down, and they began a communion service. Their heads were bowed, and I could hear some people praying. Some stood up and thanked God for their salvation, some praised God for their sins being forgiven, some just uttered words of praise and exultation to the name of Jesus Christ. I felt even worse. Let me escape this environment.

Then a man who was sitting at the front stood to his feet and began to speak. He was not reciting Scripture or praying, but he appeared to be speaking to someone. I then began to realise that the words applied to me. It was as though he had a book of my life. He knew that I was embezzling my firm, he knew that I despised my mother and treated her abominably, he understood the drunken carousing life that I was living, about the three women that I was going out with—none knowing about the other—and living a life of lies and deception.

Then for the first time in my life, I realized I was in the presence of a holy and righteous God, a God who knew every detail of my life, and the fear of the Lord came upon me. I wanted to crawl under the chair in front of me to escape from the presence of this righteous Lord, and as the man continued to speak, I prayed that the ground would open up and swallow me from the presence of this holy God.

Then as he came to the end, he said these words: "Young man, if you will give your life to Christ, He will forgive you, and He will never ever fail you throughout your life." As those words entered into my soul, I began to weep. As a strong young man, the sobs burst out from me, and I said to the Lord, "If you can love me in that way, you can have my life, and I will never fail you." At that moment, it was as though a ton of weight fell from my shoulders. I felt I was lifted off the ground and was floating a meter above its surface. The love of God flooded my being and the joy of knowing that my sins, which were many, were all washed away impacted my being like a shaft of brilliant light, flooding the darkened cell of my life. I left the church that morning a new creation, a new being, a new person. Changed so radically that I can truly say, I am still floating a meter off the ground. The words of the hymn writer, Charles Wesley, come to mind.

Long my imprisoned spirit lay,
Fast bound in sin and nature's night;
Thine eye diffused a quickening ray,
I woke; the dungeon flamed with light;
My chains fell off, my heart was free,
I rose, went forth, and followed Thee.

Since that moment of accepting Christ, truly I have risen, gone forth, and followed Christ, my life completely changed and revolutionized by His great love and mercy shown to me.

The next morning at work, I was so excited, so changed, so radically different that when the twenty young men who worked in my office had all arrived at 9:10 a.m., I jumped on one of the tables, called them all to attention and said, "Guys, I want to tell you I have given my life to Jesus and I will never be the person you knew again."

This was followed by laughter and throwing paper at me and saying, "It won't last a week." Well, it has lasted into my sixth decade of salvation and sees no end to my love and faithfulness to Jesus Christ, my Lord and Saviour. He truly has become the foundation of all my being, the Alpha and Omega of my life, the beginning and the end. And my intention is to serve Him with the last breath in my body until my friend and Saviour calls me home.

Chapter 3

You can imagine the joy in my family when I told them that I had given my life to Christ and that I would be a different person from now on. The lost sheep of the family was now in the fold, and what a huge joy that was to my brother, sister, mother and father. A life changed again in the Cunningham household. The church in Walthamstow, at my brother's request, had prayed for my salvation for many years, and when they discovered that at last I had come home, many of them were absolutely over the moon.

Paul's future father-in-law, the minister of the church, knew a good deal about me, and so in the week following, he asked to see me. He questioned me about my previous life and when discovering the nature of my lifestyle before my conversion he said to me, "Peter, when you come to church, I want you to sit in the front row. I do not want you to pray out loud, to testify, to read the Scriptures or do anything publicly for the next three months, until I can see that you are really saved and born again of the Spirit of God." Then he said to me, "Do you really want to be a successful Christian?" Of course, the answer was a resounding "Yes!" This change that had taken place was buzzing 'round me like a fire in my spirit. I wanted to run in a thousand directions to serve Jesus to the best of my ability. I could not contain the excitement of salvation.

Then he gave me this advice, "If you want to become a successful Christian, you need to talk to Jesus every day. You need to read about Jesus every day and read the Book from cover to cover. To tell about Jesus every day and to fellowship with other Christians as often as you can is life, and the lack of fellowship is death. Start reading the New Testament and treat this as God's love letter to you. This will show you how much Jesus loves you and how He wants you to live your life. It also will teach you some of the great and precious promises that are yours. You are now part of the family of God and a son of the living God."

I was eager to take up his advice because becoming a successful Christian was now the number one priority in my life, but to keep silent was almost an impossibility. I was bursting at the seams to tell anybody and everybody about the change in my life. How could I keep silent about such a wonderful person who had entered my life and changed me so radically? I prayed in desperation, "Oh God, please, please help me to remain silent in this church, and give me some way of expressing Your love to others."

One way I found was easy. I was going out with three women at the same time hoping to make sexual conquests of them all. Now that my life had changed, the only thing I could think about was how to bring them to a knowledge of my lovely Lord. So that week, Rita, Bunty, and Linda all had the revelation that I was going out with them and two other women, and that I had now given my life to Jesus Christ. I told them I would like them to attend church on Sunday with me. Rita was disgusted and angry and said she wanted nothing more to do with me, but Linda and Bunty both agreed to come to church with me that following Sunday evening. In that service, I sat there with one sitting on one side of me and one on the other side of me. I was so proud that I had brought two people to hear the Gospel preached and have the opportunity of coming to know Christ. All I can say is that Linda remained, continued to come to church and eventually, she was the first soul that I brought to know the Lord Jesus. She became my wife.

Within ten days of my salvation, I discovered another Christian young man working in the Stock Exchange who introduced me to another dozen or so young men who all loved the Lord and were passionate about serving God. They ranged in age from eighteen to twenty-five. Twice every week, they met at lunchtime to pray in one of the large, old Anglican churches where we would climb into the gallery and fall on our knees. We prayed for those who we worked with, those in our churches, those who were our bosses, and for all manner of other things in general. The church would resound with the sound of loud praying and praising and singing of choruses. I felt like I was in heaven with these young men who were so passionate about serving God. Their love for Christ encouraged me to want to fulfill the purpose of Christ in my life, and they showed me how that the Lord

Jesus had a purpose for every one of our lives if we would be only willing to be obedient to Him.

One of them, a six foot two, passionate young man for Christ, with black hair and blue eyes, named John Strickland, was running a youth work in Loughton, which was about four miles across the Essex border from my home. He asked if I would like to go and help him. I said that I thought I would be no good at working with young people, to which he replied, "Don't worry, just come and see what we do. It may encourage you." So, for a number of months, I caught the bus and went to Loughton. It was truly wonderful to see young people coming to the Lord Jesus in that work.

On a third lunchtime every week, our group of young men would go to Tower Hill. This is a place where an old part of the City Wall of London was exposed. It was about three feet high and about five feet wide. Here people would gather to talk about their politics, the reason for life, or why to be an atheist. The Christian group gathered to preach about the love of Christ and give out leaflets that were printed by a company called Victory Outreach. What excitement that was to me as a new Christian, to hear these young men speak so eloquently about their faith. It filled me with joy to hear one after another climb up on the wall and confess their faith in Jesus Christ. Often a small crowd would gather, and we had an opportunity to witness to some of those that stood to hear.

In the fourth week, I stood there with them thoroughly enjoying what was taking place. I am only five feet seven inches, as thin as a chip and weighing only nine stone. Two of the young men, both six-footers, suddenly grabbed me by both arms and threw me up on the wall and said, "Come on, Pete. It's your turn." I looked out across the crowd that had gathered, and with a swelling sense of Christ being present with me, I blurted out at the top of my voice, "Believe in the Lord Jesus Christ and thou shalt be saved." I jumped down off the wall and felt like I had conquered the planet. There could not be a higher moment of excitement and joy in my being ever again in my life. I had publicly testified of my faith in Jesus Christ.

Week after week, we joined together to pray, and week after week, I loved to climb upon London's thousand-year-old wall and testify of my faith in Jesus Christ. As the weeks and months passed by, the Lord gave me a greater confidence as well as a greater knowledge of the Scriptures, and we saw many people gather 'round as we began to preach to them.

I also began to attend the youth work as I had been invited to go. It looked after the 18 to 30-year-olds, and about forty of us would gather on a Friday evening. Sometimes we had visiting preachers, and I just could not get enough of hearing the work of God. On Tuesdays, we had a prayer meeting at the church where forty to fifty people would gather. Most of us had been baptized in the Holy Ghost and spoke in other tongues, so we would have messages in tongues, interpretations and prophecies, all just exciting me more. Thursdays was the Bible study where we had an associate minister, Fred Howes. He must have been seventy-five if he was a day, and on the third, fourth, or fifth Bible study, he was preaching on us being patient to see the will of God fulfilled in our lives. He quoted a Scripture that I have remembered to this day. *Line upon line, precept upon precept, here a little, there a little.*

At the tender age of twenty-one, I wanted to complete all that God had for me by the time I was twenty-two. I was in a desperate hurry to get on with the work of the Kingdom and extremely impatient to do the will of God. I have learnt over the past sixty years that God had a plan for my life, and it is only over the last decade I have seen the purpose of God beginning to be truly fulfilled in my life. He had prepared an amazing work for me to do. I heard one preacher say that it is better to be used for one day in the perfect will of God than to strive fifty years to serve Him in your own strength. After fifty years, truly that day has come.

Chapter 4

I have never found hearing the voice of God difficult or complex. It just seems to be a natural part of knowing God, loving God, serving God and being personally acquainted with Him.

The first four months of my salvation seemed to fly by. I loved to get up early at 6:30 a.m. and seek the face of God and read the Scriptures, and in late April of 1964, one of the young men in the church I was attending came and asked if I would like to go to a Christian conference on the second weekend of May. He told me it would be a wonderful experience for me and that it would be like going to heaven for a weekend. Thousands of Christians would be there, they would be singing like the choirs of heaven, the preachers would be world-renowned and would bless my socks off and the presence of God would be so good, it would be hard to move. So, with that recommendation, I readily accepted the invitation.

On the Friday evening that I arrived to stay at his flat overnight, he was working under the bonnet of his car. For some unknown reason, the vehicle would not start. He spent an hour taking wires on and off, cleaning the carburetor, taking the spark plugs in and out, but it still would not work.

So, at about 9:30 p.m., he closed the bonnet and said that we will just have to hand it over to the Lord.

By 10 p.m., as we prepared to go to bed, he said that we need to pray that the car will be fixed by the morning. So, dropping to my knees by the bed, in my heart I thought, "This is going to need some great intercession to make the car work." Dennis then prayed out loud, "Lord, you know what is wrong with my car, how we cannot get it to start. You are the Creator of all things, so just put it right for us." He promptly jumped into bed. I thought to myself, "That is a real prayer of faith." So, I climbed into an old wooden chair bed and spent an uncomfortable night on some very lumpy cushions.

We were up at 6:30 a.m., and by 7 a.m., we were out packing our cases into the car. I was mystified as the night previously, the car had refused to start. We climbed in, my friend into the driving seat and me into the passenger seat, and then I saw an extraordinary act of faith. My friend prayed, "God, I thank You that You always hear our prayers. Please make this car start in Jesus' name." He pressed the start button, the engine burst into life, and this old, split-screen 1953 Morris Minor moved off gently. We were on our way to Clacton-on-Sea.

The place we were staying was a cottage about four miles outside the town. We arrived at about 2:30 p.m., settled in and then departed for the conference centre for the first of the meetings we were to attend. It was totally mind-blowing to see about 5,000 Christians all meeting in one place and then beginning to sing worship and praise choruses. It was like being transported to heaven, just as my friend said.

The Bible reading was from Isaiah 9. I can remember the words: "His name shall be called Wonderful Counsellor, Mighty God..." Then the preacher got up to preach. There must have been more than a dozen people sitting on the platform with him. He began to speak about the titles of Christ, and the more he spoke, the more the auditorium became filled with the presence of the Holy Ghost. It seemed that God's anointing rested on His servant, and the more he preached, the more the anointing increased until we felt we could not move because of the presence of God. At last, the preacher said, "I feel I must sit down because of the presence of God." The people on the platform said if you sit down, we must stand up. So he sat down, and they stood up and began to worship God until the whole congregation erupted into praise and worship of the living God. For about an hour, the worship of the Almighty continued, and as the meeting ended, I just felt that I needed to walk 'round the campsite as the presence of God seemed to rest on us all.

Arriving back about midnight, I fell asleep until my alarm woke me at 6 a.m. on Sunday. I arose, washed and dressed, and I had bought myself a very large, wide-margin Bible which, on many occasions, I hugged to myself as I told Jesus that I loved Him. So, on this May morning, I took my Bible and hugged it as I crossed the meadow by the cottage and set out to read and pray. The sun was up, it was a beautiful, cloudless May morning, the birds were singing, and my heart skipped as I talked to my Lord as I walked. I sat down on a riverbank and opened the Scriptures. I had started reading the New Testament, a chapter a day, and I was in the book of Romans, having read the four gospels and the book of Acts.

After I finished reading, I just meditated and talked to the Lord and then, for the first time in my Christian life, I heard God's voice speak within me. The Lord said, "Peter, I want you to serve Me." I replied, "Lord, I cannot serve You, I am only a child." The Lord spoke to me again, "Peter, I want you to serve Me." I said, "Ah, Lord God, how can I serve You? I am but a babe." Then the voice of the Lord spoke again, "Read Jeremiah." Then like Sarah, I laughed. I said within myself, "There is no such book as Jeremiah. This is just my imagination." I turned to the front of my Bible and looked down the table of contents. I looked down the first column and there was no such book called Jeremiah. I began to look down the second column, and there in the centre, to my astonishment, was the book of Jeremiah. My mind questioned, "What shall I do?" So, I thought I better start at the beginning.

I began to read the first chapter of Jeremiah, and soon came upon a few verses where Jeremiah is spoken to by the Lord: "Jeremiah, I want you to speak for Me." Jeremiah's response was, "Ah, Lord God, I am but a child." Exactly as I had answered the Lord! I was totally amazed and absorbed in this scripture. God goes on in the chapter to say, "Don't be afraid of their faces, I will put My word in your mouth."

This was amazing to see how God understood and knew me altogether, for when I had started my employment in stockbroking, I had been a Messenger Boy. I had to take transfer documents for our office to the HMRC office to pay stamp duty on share transactions. I also had to deliver other documents to other stockbroking firms. Suddenly, everything in my mind came so clear. "I will put My word in your mouth," God was saying to me, "I just want you to be My messenger boy." I thought to myself, "Yes, God, I can be a messenger boy. I can take Your word, not my word, to whoever and wherever You send me." For over fifty years now, I have just been a messenger boy for the Almighty.

As I stood up and began to walk from that riverbank, in the simplicity of my faith, I imagined my God coming down to speak to Jeremiah, putting His arm 'round his shoulder and saying to him, "Jeremiah, I want you to pen these words because in 3,000 years' time, a young man will argue with Me about the service I will call him to. And when he has argued, I will point him to the words that you have penned and tell him that all I want to do is put My word in his mouth and for him to go to whoever I send him."

God has sent me to some amazing people during my life, and that promise God made me when I was a Christian of four and a half months has been fulfilled a hundred times over. I bless my God for His grace and mercy and for privileging me to be His servant. Of course, I now realise that God was speaking to Jeremiah and that Jeremiah was like I had been on that day: doubtful about his ability, unsure about his pedigree, and not understanding that God was capable of doing amazing things through those who were willing to serve Him. It reminds me of the Scripture that says, "He takes the fools to confound the wise and the weak to confound the mighty" (My paraphrase of 1 Corinthians 1:27 KJV).

Do you feel you are weak, inadequate and without ability? Then you are just the type of person that God can take and use if you are willing just to be a messenger boy. Whatever He speaks into your heart, you take to those He sends you to and deliver His message of Truth and Righteousness.

Chapter 5

As a result of sitting on the riverbank on that May day, many things began to change in the following twelve months, of which we do not have time to mention them all. However, here are three of them:

The call to youth work, which blew me away.

The call to give up ten of my beautiful suits to missionaries leaving the Congo as the revolution began there, which was a great privilege.

The call to become a herald, which excited me.

Let us start with the call to youth work. In July of 1964, I was approached by our youth leader. By that time, Linda had come to know Christ, and we were attending church regularly, going to the youth group catering for ages eighteen plus on a Friday, the prayer meeting on a Tuesday, the Bible study on a Thursday, communion on Sunday morning and the Gospel service on Sunday evening. One Sunday evening after church, when our youth group had gathered in one of the homes to have supper and sing choruses, I was approached by our youth leader. He said, "I feel we need a junior youth group catering for twelve to seventeen-year-olds, and I feel that Paul and Hazel and you and Linda should be leading that group. I would love you to pray about it."

The idea to me appeared ludicrous. I had been a Christian for seven months, my life prior to coming to Christ had been anything but exemplary and knowing that I had a violent temper, the idea of me looking after kids filled me with horror. I thought to myself, "I am sure they will annoy me; my patience will fail, and I am liable to be hitting one of them. Our youth leader has picked the wrong person. I will help to bring a bad reputation to our church as an uncaring, unfeeling group of people that has no interest in children." However, was I going to refuse this? At first I told him it was a crazy idea, that it couldn't be the Lord who had spoken to him. He didn't know my character, and I would do those young people more harm than good, but he insisted that the Lord had spoken to him of the four of us doing this work.

My mind had still not lost its ability to scheme and plot. I thought, "I know how I can get out of this; I will go and see Pastor Norman. He knows my character inside out. He will see the folly of our youth leader's ways and will speak to him and point out the error of his ways." I made an appointment to see my pastor before the end of the week. On entering his study, he said, "Let us pray before we begin to speak." So, he prayed that God would give us wisdom in the matter that we were about to discuss. I explained to him that our youth leader had been to see me and asked me to begin to run a new youth work catering for twelve to seventeen-year-olds. This would be in conjunction with Linda, Paul and Hazel, and the four of us would have joint responsibility. Then I reminded him that we had spoken at length about my character and how he knew that I had a violent temper and could be provoked easily. As youngsters of this age would undoubtedly bring problems, this was an extremely bad request for me to be running a youth group.

He leaned back in his chair and carefully considered the words that he would deliver to me. Norman came from the small town of Bishop Auckland, situated in County Durham, and still used some of the endearing local ways of speaking when wanting to convey a message of love and understanding. He opened by saying, "Ah bonny lad, I am going to tell you something now that was told to me when I first became a Christian. This good Christian man said to me when I had doubts about serving Christ, 'Bonny lad, if someone asks you to do something for Jesus, always say yes. If you are no good at it, they won't ask you again.'" What could I say when being answered in such a way? Therefore, I agreed to take on the work that had been offered to me.

Let me say that we do not know what lays latent within our temperament, within our character, within the inner recesses of our heart and mind, but God does, and He knew that working with young people was something that He had ordained for me to do for many years. So, the work commenced. Five young people grew to ten, ten grew to twenty, twenty grew to forty, and on a Monday evening, we would gather to play, to sing and to talk to these young people about their need for Jesus Christ.

From its very beginning, I would travel home from work

on Monday night, go to my bedroom and on the door of one of the cupboards, I pinned a list of names that grew continually. They were the names of the young people that began to come to that weekly meeting, and every Monday night, I would fall on my knees, weep and say, "God, if you do not help me tonight, I am lost," and I would pray over every name that God would help us to draw these young people into a knowledge of Him.

In the next eighteen months, we saw most of them come to a knowledge of the Lord Jesus. Some of them have gone into ministry: some of them have developed into youth workers or Sunday school workers or have gone into church leadership. All I can say is that God made that ministry fruitful. He was the head and the tail. He was surely the Alpha and Omega of all that we achieved in that wonderful time.

Let me move on to when I gave away ten of my beautiful suits. As I have already said, when I came to Christ, I was a snappy dresser, having twelve wonderful suits in my wardrobe. As we came to the end of 1964 and the beginning of 1965, a mission called the Congo Evangelical Mission, which had pioneered some 700 churches in the Congo since the middle of the 1930s, faced a great upheaval as the Congo Civil War broke out. Some of the missionaries lost their lives, and many others fled in just their shirts and shorts and the women in their dresses. All of their possessions were lost, and they returned to the UK totally bereft of all worldly goods. My heart was moved and stirred as we prayed and fasted for the deliverance of these good and godly people.

I was challenged in my spirit as to what we could do to help them in such conditions. We had financially given as a church far above our normal giving to help relieve the stress that they were going through. I determined in my heart that I needed to do more, but what could I do?

Then I felt as though the Lord prompted me, "You have twelve beautiful suits in your wardrobe. Do you really need them all?" My heart was stirred, and I knew that this was the right thing to do. So, I went upstairs to my bedroom and opened the wardrobe doors. I thrust my arms in, gathered up ten of those suits, took them downstairs, placed them on the back seat of a little battered Austin A30—which had become our chariot of love to the community—and drove 'round to Pastor Norman's house.

Lifting the bundle of suits from the back seat, I knocked on his door, and when his face appeared, I thrust the suits forward and said, "Pastor, these are for the Congo missionaries who have left their mission with nothing. I hope these suits will be okay for some of them."

When I left, a sense of joy rose within my spirit and belief that these suits would be a blessing to those wonderful people who had run for their lives at such an awful time in their existence. Serving God costs us at times, and for me, that was costly but wonderful knowing it had pleased my Lord and would be of benefit to His Kingdom.

Finally, number three. I want to mention what happened in June of 1965. When I had been to the conference in May of 1964, the leaders of our group of churches had spoken of young men and women giving up a year of their lives to help some of the smaller churches in our movement. All they would guarantee to those young men and women was a bed where they may lay their head and the cost of the fare to reach the destination of the church they were appointed to. They would be required to do whatever the bidding of the local minister was. It could be helping with evangelism, helping with Sunday school, helping to clean or decorate the church, engaging in renovations, knocking on the doors and inviting people to attend the church or giving out leaflets inviting people to come to the church. No matter what was requested of the heralds, for that is what they were called, they were to carry out the task.

I must admit, when hearing about this in May of 1964, my heart was stirred because all I wanted to do was to serve the Lord Jesus. In May of 1965, two young men came to our church who were on the Herald Mission Scheme. I felt so challenged that I should be doing this work and felt in my spirit that I needed to apply to be a herald. I began to pray that God would guide me and that I would, if it were His will, take up this challenge.

Now at the beginning of June, our pastor was going away on holiday and he had invited a minister to come and take the Sunday services. I had recently read about Gideon and how when he was not sure, he put a fleece out to test the will of God. I thought, "Lord, I am going to put a fleece out to see if you really want me to become a herald. This man who is coming and who is going to preach, I want him to come to me personally and say, 'Young man, God wants you to serve Him full-time.' If he does that, then I will know with certainty that this is what you want me to do." So, the next Sunday he came and preached on the Sunday morning but not on anything to do with serving God full-time.

As a church at that moment in time, we were running five Sunday schools, and I was a teacher in one of those Sunday schools called Priory Court. As usual, I arrived at the church early, and as I was not doing any of the practical games that we did at the beginning of Sunday school, I sat at the back. The preacher arrived at the Sunday school and, to my amazement, came and sat next to me. He then nudged me and said, "I wanted to talk to you."

You can imagine how my heart leapt. I think it was doing 200 beats per minute. The preacher had said he wanted to talk to me! This could only be to tell me that God wanted me to serve Him full-time. I looked him in the face, and his next words completely deflated all my expectations. His next sentence was, "I understand you know where to buy the best secondhand tires," which is true because in 1965, all our cars were old, and any new parts that I needed came from the breakers yard. Also, when new tires were required, they were again from the breakers yard. I advised him where the best secondhand tire dealer was, and he left Sunday school a very satisfied man.

In the evening, he preached a magnificent sermon on serving God full-time. Again my heart pounded, and at the end, he made an appeal and said, "I believe there are young people here who should be serving God full-time." My head was in my hands, my eyes were tightly shut, and I said, "God, this is not the way I asked. I cannot respond." Then he said, "I see that hand, I see that young person responding. God will bless you and honour you."

We sang our closing hymn, and I went and collected an old couple called the Archers who I was taking home in my car. We left quickly after the service. I took them home and then returned to the church to collect Linda for us to go home to her house together. I parked outside the front entrance of the building, and as I sat there waiting for Linda to come out, the preacher came out, and standing on the corner, looking up and down the street as though to get his bearings and see where he had parked his car, saw me sitting there in my car. He came over and knocked on the window.

I wound it down and he said, "Young man, that was for you."

I looked up into his face and asked, "What was for me?"

He replied, "God wants you to serve Him full-time."

I felt like everything exploded at once. I could not contain myself that the dear Almighty, Lord of Creation, had deigned to send a message from Himself confirming that I was to be a servant of the living God.

When Linda got into the car, the first thing she said to me was, "That was amazing!"

I thought, "How does she know?"

I said, "What was amazing?"

She said, "It was me who put my hand up."

On arriving home, my Scripture reading for that night was Galatians 5:1. The words still resound in my mind today: "Stand firm therefore in the liberty where Christ has made you free and be not entangled in the yoke of bondage."

I would never put a fleece out again or doubt the Almighty, and so it has been. When His word has been spoken into my heart, I have acted upon it. Sometimes more slowly than I should have done but never another fleece.

When God speaks to you, don't doubt it. Always move forward in faith, for He will never fail you.

Chapter 6

The very next day, I was ready to pack my bags and enter full-time service for the Almighty. Of course, it didn't happen that way. First of all, my pastor returned, and after some discussion and my telling him of the amazing experience I had, he put me in touch with the head of our home missions and approved my application, which was duly sent. After being interviewed and receiving confirmation of my acceptance, I received my first appointment of service as a herald for the Home Missions of the AOG (Assemblies of God), Great Britain and Northern Ireland, in February 1966. It was with a small church in Dundee, Scotland, and I was amazed that I was being sent so far away.

My realization of this great challenge that now awaited me began to dawn upon my own innermost being. I was leaving my family behind, I was leaving my church behind, and I was leaving Linda behind. I had given up my job, I had no income, and now God was sending me to what appeared to be the uttermost parts of the earth. There was a wavering in my spirit and, thinking of my previous life before I had become a Christian, I asked the Lord, "Are you sending me there to die?" I prayed that God would help me on the journey and reserved a seat on the train. When the ticket arrived for the journey to Dundee, I packed my case, waved goodbye to those who came to see me off and found my seat.

A man entered the carriage where I was sitting. It was a man I had seen before. He was one of the leaders of our movement, a man called Steven Page, who loved God ardently and served Him with a passion. I could not believe that God had put this godly man opposite me on my train journey to Dundee. He was travelling further than I. He was going to Aberdeen to a convention that was being held there that weekend.

How my heart burned on that eight-hour journey as he spoke to me of the things of God, of ministry, and of our service to Christ. So much wisdom seemed to flow from his lips that when I got to Dundee, I knew with certainty that I was in the centre of God's will for what He had called me to be. My arrival there brought into sharp focus, however, that what God had called us to do would have to be a labour of love. For when I left the station, the rain was falling, and if anyone has been to Dundee, they will now understand my description of my first impressions of that city. The sky was grey, the buildings that surrounded the station were all built out of grey granite, and the minister arrived in a grey van. It was as though I had arrived in a city where everything was in white, grey, or black.

On arriving at the house that I was staying in, I met another herald called John Cox who became perhaps the closest friend I ever had. I was welcomed into the home and given tea and a slice of toast with beans on. Later, in the room we would be sharing, I said to John that it was very kind of our host to give me those beans on toast when I just arrived. He said to me, "That is the normal tea. The lady here has a domestic science degree and knows how many calories we need to eat so don't expect a great deal of food." I replied, "Surely not." Then he took a pair of trousers and showed me where they had been taken in. He said, "I have been here three months and have lost a stone and a half." The next day would prove that what he had told me was absolutely correct.

The next day was a Sunday, and we had the service followed by Sunday school. As a young man, I was certainly able to eat a horse when I became hungry. At about 2 p.m., forty-five minutes before lunchtime, we returned home. On opening the door, the smell of roast beef was pungent in the air and the gastric juices began to flow. The table was set, and we were called to eat. There were tureens on the table and a piece of beef which was one of those round pieces of beef, maybe ten centimeters in diameter but only four centimeters deep. I looked at it and thought, "I could put that piece of beef on two slices of bread and eat all of it myself." But it was to feed three grown men, two sons and the wife! We were also short of potatoes and vegetables. We certainly had sufficient calories to sustain body and soul but nothing that would put meat on our bones.

This led us in the following months, as we were called to do door-to-door visitation, to look for other means of sustenance. We took note of houses that offered tea and biscuits or cake or a sandwich and made it a point to return at least once a week to supplement our diet. Perhaps we were not the most humble of servants, but we felt we were the neediest of servants. We had a wonderful time also redecorating the church inside and out, seeking to serve God by following all the instructions of the leadership.

I was then moved to Ayre, Scotland where John followed me two weeks later. We lived with a family where the father was the mate on an inshore fishing boat. It was there I contracted chickenpox, which was a dreadful experience from which I thought I would die. I learnt some Scottish expressions such as where the mother would say she was going to "scelp the weans," and take a "curren of sweeties," and a young lady was referred to as a hen. The food was amazing, the mother of the house was friendly and lovely and godly, and her husband would take us out for two days on fishing trips. It was amazing to see the net come up bulging with fish. They would pull the string at the bottom of the net and the fish would cascade onto the deck resulting in us standing there in twenty centimeters of fish slushing 'round our feet. I loved the fact that Jesus said He would make us fishers of men. I hoped to see the nets that we cast as full of men and women as these nets were full of fish.

The AOG church in Ayre did not have a pastor, so John and I were left to organise things in some ways. This was a wonderful experience. There was a congregation of about seventeen, and so we started a youth and children's work, which began to flourish. A number of the congregation who had left the church began to return including two young men who had backslidden. The church grew in the next five months to nearly forty. Then I was called away and John was left. By the time he moved from Ayre, they had established a leadership team, and the church grew to 150 folk meeting regularly.

Some time later, John and I had the privilege of returning to visit and see the church fully operational with a new pastor as the leader of the church. While I was there, we visited a group of young people in Glasgow. I don't think that up to that time I had come across such a passionate group of young people. We went to a prayer time to share our testimonies. They sang with such love and passion for Christ, and we got to see souls brought into the Kingdom. One chorus from that time has remained with me throughout my life. The words were:

Lead me to some soul today,
O teach me, Lord, just what to say;
Friends of mine are lost in sin,
And cannot find their way.
Few there are who seem to care,
And few there are who pray;
Melt my heart and fill my life,
Give me one soul today.

As we sang this over and over, the tears rolled down my cheeks as the longing to see the hearts of men and women turning to Christ gripped my heart. That experience is as alive today as it was then in my memory.

Let me tell you the final chapter of my friendship with John Cox. After spending some nine months together, John returned home. When I returned home after two years with my church in Walthamstow, I was meeting with my first pastor, Norman Young, in his home. The phone rang and it was for me. It was John's father. The news that he gave me broke my heart. John and his brother Peter had been returning home from playing football, and both of them had been killed in a road accident. I left the room and paced up and down in the corridor of my pastor's house. The expression that Jesus used in John 14:16 became a reality to me that day. In this chapter, Jesus said he will send us a Comforter. As I paced up and down, suddenly the Holy Ghost came upon me and I began to speak in other tongues and to magnify the God of our creation, and I realised the reality of that scripture. Whether we live or die, we are the Lord's.

Ten days later, I stood on the hillside cemetery just outside Louth in Lincolnshire, England. Some three or four hundred people had gathered 'round the open graves and as the coffins were laid, someone began to sing.

There is going to be a meeting in the air,
In the sweet, sweet bye and bye.
I am going to meet you, meet you over there,
In that home beyond the sky.
Such singing you will hear never heard by mortal ear,
'Twill be glorious, I do declare.

And God's own son will be the leading one,
At the meeting in the air.

John was just two months short of his nineteenth birthday, and his brother Peter was just seventeen. I felt like I was on Victoria Station waving goodbye to my friend John with a sure and certain hope of the resurrection to life eternal. This memory brings tears to my eyes even as I pen these words. I am going to see my closest friend in that home that Christ has prepared for those that love Him.

From Ayre, I was sent by the AOG Home Missions to work on a crusade in Scarborough, England. The evangelist was a wonderful man called Ron Hickling, and what continually amused me about him was that he knew the Scriptures so well. When preaching, he would open the Bible at random usually to the middle around the book of Psalms and then quote the scriptures from the New Testament.

It always tickled me as I knew he wasn't reading from the Bible but quoting it and looking like he was reading. We saw a number of people come to know the Lord Jesus while we were there, and the joy of seeing that church grow was fabulous. I was duly sent from Scarborough to a crusade in Ripon. From Ripon to a crusade that was held in Wigan where I first saw the amazing power of the Holy Ghost healing many people.

The evangelist at this crusade was Melvyn Banks, and the town had about 40,000 houses in it. The church was about thirty strong, and the minister, Ray Belfield, was so keen to see people come to Christ and see the church grow that about six heralds, including myself, were sent to give out about 80,000 leaflets inviting people to the crusade. The church building was new and had only just been completed. The hall, with a balcony now, held about 250 people, and it was to this venue that we invited people.

Melvyn Banks was amazingly blessed by the Almighty with gifts of healing and it soon became evident when the crusade had started that this was shown in his ministry. The first few nights we had maybe fifty to sixty people attending. On the third night, which was a Wednesday, a lady with multiple-sclerosis was brought by her husband with her children in a wheelchair. Melvyn Banks prayed for her, and she pushed the wheelchair out of the church. The local newspaper, *The Observer*, printed the story on that Friday, and on the Saturday night, the church was full to capacity after folk had read of this miraculous event that had taken place.

Let me relate a healing miracle that affected me the most at this crusade. One of the duties of a herald was to stand with the evangelist as he prayed for those who were sick and had come for healing. On that particular evening, a family called the Walters came. The father was completely deaf and, from what I recall, had never been able to hear. He sat on the front row of the church with his wife and daughter seated behind him. His daughter was thirteen, a very beautiful girl. The preacher came to her father and asked him what his problem was. Mr. Walters gestured to his ears, telling the evangelist that he was deaf and could not hear.

So, Melvyn put his fingers in the man's ears and prayed and then he whispered into one of his ears, "Jesus loves you." The man responded as if he had heard something, and so the preacher put his fingers in the man's ears again and prayed again ardently that the Lord Jesus would heal this man of his deafness. He then whispered into the man's ear again, "Say, 'Jesus.'" The man responded and said, "Jesus." The preacher whispered in his ear again, "Say, 'Jesus loves me.'" He said, "Jesus loves me."

Suddenly, I saw the expression on his daughter's face. It was just amazing. Her face lit up, ignited by the fact that her father had repeated what the preacher had said to him and said, "Dad, can you really hear?" The man replied without turning his head, "Jeanie, is that really you?" For the first time in his life, he heard his daughter's voice. Tears are in my eyes now as they filled my eyes on that day. I couldn't stand with the preacher any longer as the emotion of seeing God heal this man and him hear his lovely daughter for the first time just overtook me. I had to go to the back of the church and just weep with joy after seeing the good hand of God heal this man totally and absolutely from his deafness. This would be the first of a number of healings that I have been blessed to experience during my Christian life.

My final experience of being a herald in those two years and travelling the length and breadth of the country was to be introduced to a children and youth camp that Ray Belfield and another minister, Bob Stevenson, had set up called Bonsall Holiday Camp. This was situated in a small village in the Derbyshire Peak District, called Bonsall, just above the town of Matlock. I will talk more of this later.

Chapter 7

On the completion of my service as a herald, I returned to Walthamstow as a full-time helper at Emmanuel Hall Church under the tutelage of Pastor Norman Young. During this year, Linda and I were married. Prior to the wedding, I had an amazing experience of the provisions of the Almighty take place in respect to my wedding suit.

Earlier, I shared about the time I donated ten of my suits to the missionaries returning home from the Congo. This just left me with two suits, which were not the best of the bunch. By the time I returned home from my exploits as a herald in January 1969 and prepared for my marriage in March, both of my suits were in a sorry state, with patches on the seat of the trousers. In faith, I went to Burtons and put a deposit on a made-to-measure suit that cost £15. I said, "Lord, I have never asked you for anything for myself, but it would be nice to look smart on my wedding day." I committed my way into the hands of the Almighty.

One of the things that Norman had taught me was to be a handyman, and so my brother and I were asked to help decorate the home of the Archers, an elderly couple in their late seventies. With joy in my heart and a skip in my step, I helped to paint the doors and skirting boards and re-wall-paper their front room. If I say so myself, it looked fabulous when we finished, and on leaving the home on that final evening, Mrs. Archer pressed a small brown envelope into my hands. On arriving home, I opened the envelope. Inside were fifteen £1 notes and a little note. Written on the page were these words, "The Lord has told me to give you this for your suit." The tears flowed as I rejoiced in the goodness of God.

There were three things that Norman Young really wanted me to be engaged in. The first was the upkeep of the church and its buildings, the second was visiting members of the congregation, and the third was looking after the junior youth work once again. Norman Young was absolutely fabulous to work with—loving and understanding, passionate about telling others about Christ, and a work ethic that was second to none. He would put himself out to help anybody who came with a need. I remember him taking the minibus all the way to Norfolk to help someone in difficulty.

Because of his working-class upbringing, he was very practical and would often save the church money by doing some of the building works himself. I can remember that summer, we had bought two houses next to the church, and the chimney pots needed to be removed. Talk about scary experiences. The thought of clambering on a roof to take down four 3-foot chimney pots still gives me goosebumps. Somehow we managed to achieve the objectives, and as far as I remember, he sold the chimney pots as garden ornaments. Norman never missed the opportunity of making a profit for the church.

Let me now talk to you about working with the youth group. After being with the group for three months, about twenty of them had really come to know the Lord, and being that one of my great motivations was to pray and read the Scriptures, my desire to have these young people follow this model was quite intense. So, I began to pray with a number of them and read the Scriptures twice a week before they went to school. Five or six of them began to join me on these days and three of them—Karen, Kenny, and Patrick—became really passionate about seeing their school friends come to Christ. They all went to different high schools and that summer had moved into the GCSE class. I encouraged them to see if we could open a Christian Union in each of their schools. To my delight, by the end of September, we were meeting regularly at lunchtime in each of the schools. By the end of November, the five senior high schools had Christian Unions running in them.

With a desire to bring them all together so that we could truly be the Body of Christ, I invited all the Christian Union members to pray together once a week at a local church hall in the centre of Walthamstow. The hall had a wood burner stove in the middle of the room with a metal flue going up through the roof. I would arrive early and set the fire going in the stove, and then around twenty or thirty youngsters would turn up to pray for their schools and for young men and women to know Jesus. What an awesome time this was, what an inspiring time this was, what a challenging time this was as the prayers of these young people broke through into heaven when they cried to the Lord to see many of their friends come to Christ.

It so happened that we decided in December that we would invite all the schools to come together the following February. We would ask a Christian band to come and play gospel music and testify their faith in Christ to the young people who would gather at the event. We designed posters, one of which showed a young person in a tin can being replicated many times on a conveyor belt and just said, "Don't be a canned man." To my overwhelming surprise, when that 1970 February Friday evening came and we met in the hall of the George Monarchs Grammar School for Boys, some three to four hundred youngsters gathered in the hall.

The testimonies were passionate, the music was great, the preacher was amazing, and at the end of the meeting, an appeal was made. I was blown away by the response. Over a hundred young people came to the front to accept Christ as Lord and Saviour. Certainly, the Lord was beginning to work among the young people in the area, and the evangelical churches were beginning to feel the effect.

In January 1970, an independent pornographic film company had bought a cinema on a major crossroads in Walthamstow and had opened it as a private club to show these films. The youngsters were incensed by having such a club open and had decided to arrange a rally in May of 1970 outside the cinema to protest its existence. I believe from these baby steps of churches working together a movement arose called Light for Life. This movement in the early seventies affected the whole of the Southeast of England and saw many churches beginning to work together to promote the Gospel of Jesus. As a result, many men and women came to know Jesus as their Lord and Saviour. I remember those days as one of the highlights of my Christian experience.

During the course of my time at Walthamstow, the summer holidays were approaching, and I asked my pastor if there was somewhere Linda and I could go to be useful during our week's holiday time. My desire always was to see people come to know Christ, and I anticipated doing something evangelistic during that period. Norman Young had a nephew working in a small church in Hertfordshire and sent us to help Stephen Young. So, off we went, my heart skipping with anticipation of winning someone for Jesus. When we arrived, Stephen said, "I am so glad you have come. I really do need some help." It seems to run in the Young family that they all were practically minded and handymen. Stephen had decided that while I was there, we could help rewire the church.

Every time I think of that church, it brings a smile to my face. The church was an old fire station, which was there to put out fires. The prayer room was the old mortuary where the dead would be laid, and their minibus for collecting people was an old ambulance. So, I'd gone to a church whose building was for putting out fires, not lighting them, whose prayer room was for accommodating the dead and not the living, and their method of bringing people to church was using a vehicle used for sick people. So, my work began to help with the rewiring of the church. My job was to fit through a small hole in the ceiling into the roof area. For five days in a really hot summer, I crawled around in the dark sweltering heat of the rafters, and we completed the job on the Friday lunchtime.

Stephen's wife was a lovely lady full of compassion and certainly a very good cook who prepared very tasty meals for us. As we sat at lunch, Steve said, "Tonight we will go out and evangelise." That was music to my ears. I'd been waiting all week to go out and evangelise. On that Friday evening, we took out some tracts in our hands and went down to the High Street. It was totally and absolutely empty, not a soul to be seen. So, we walked up and down, looking down the side streets, and on the third occasion, a young man appeared. The young man was named Bob Merritt, and of course we button-holed him and began to talk to him about Jesus. To my amazement, he became extremely interested, and on the Sunday, he came to church and gave his life to Christ. Wow, we had won a soul! It was worth all the crawling and sweating in the roof to win a soul for Jesus. Bob went on to serve the Lord Jesus, and my last contact with him was that he had been made an elder in a church in Middlesbrough in the Northeast of England.

In December of 1969, I had an unexpected phone call from Pastor Ray Belfield, whose church I had served in as a herald in the town of Wigan. He said he would like me to join him as his assistant pastor and would train me for full-time ministry. I had already been offered this position a year earlier, and during 1969, had prayed earnestly about the offer and concluded this would be the will of God for Linda and me if Ray should offer again. By now I had married, and Linda was heavily pregnant with our first child. Having prayed about Wigan before, I felt that it was right for us to take up this invitation, and I agreed with Ray that after three months' notice at Walthamstow, I would move to Wigan on April 1, 1970.

The joy of our first baby's arrival was now imminent, and on January 8, 1970, we took Linda down to the Thorpe Coombe Maternity Hospital to await the arrival of our first child. I will never understand the pain of childbirth, but I have certainly had the privilege of being at the birth of all our six children and being with Linda through those painful moments.

In Thorpe Coombe, Linda was put into a room with four other beds. She was often showing signs of distress from the labour pains and the nurses asked me to go outside while they prepared her for the delivery. On my return to sit with her, she said with delight, "They have given me this to help with the pain and it really works." I can see it now. It was gas and air, the machine had a chrome handle, a black face mask attached to the chrome handle and a black tube running into the chrome handle. Suddenly, she had one of her labour pains and instead of putting the mask to her face she lifted her arm up straight and just gripped the handle as hard as she could. Her arm was shaking as she gripped it tighter. The mask flew off, the black pipe dropped to the floor and all that was left in her hand was the chrome handle. "Oh," she said, "I have broken their machine. They will be throwing me out because of the damage I've caused." Of course, this did not happen. I scrambled around on the floor, found the black face mask and the hose and reattached them to the chrome handle. Around mid-day on January 9, 1970, our first son was born. If you remember, I have told you the story of John and his brother Paul who were killed in a car accident. I named our first son in memory of them. John Paul Cunningham had now entered the world.

We then began to prepare for our move to Wigan. When I was a herald in Wigan, the minister Ray Belfield and I had related extremely well, and he was now in the process of building a new church that had just begun construction. He and another minister, Bob Stevenson, also purchased Bonsall Holiday Camp to run as a child and youth camp during the summer holidays. So on April 1, 1970, Linda and our newborn son John and I travelled to Wigan. Our wage would be the princely sum of £3 per week (the average wage then was £12) and the promise of accommodation. This was in the home of a family that came to the church with their young son who was three months older than John. The friendship between their son Phil and our son John has lasted to the present time. They put a bed and a cot in their spare room, and this became our home.

My responsibilities were to open a work for older people called the Silver Liners, look after the youth work, help with the development and ministry of the Holiday Centre and, to my surprise, open a book shop. I also was asked to preach once a fortnight on Sunday morning and once a fortnight on Sunday evening. During my stay there, I saw the church grow from around 35 people to around 120 in a two-year period.

Living in one room and sharing a house with a family was quite difficult. As one would say, there was no room to swing a cat. At the church, one of our elders was a lady called Dora Finch. The Finch's were quite a wealthy Christian family, and Dora's brother was always interested in furthering the Kingdom of Heaven. So, Pastor Ray negotiated with him a gift to help us open a Christian book shop within the town. A property situated on Mesnes Street was rented for this purpose. On the ground floor, there was the shop premises, on the first floor was a fellowship room and on the top floor a one bedroomed flat, which was to become our home for the next twelve months.

With the help of some of the church members, we renovated the shop to put bookshelves in and made an area where four tables were placed with four chairs round each table to become our coffee lounge. On the first floor, we prepared the meeting room, and on the top floor where there was just one room, we fitted a kitchen and counter to separate the kitchen area from the living area. The bedroom was an L shape, so we added a studded wall to create a small nursery area for John. I do thank God for all the training that Norman Young gave me down in Walthamstow. The handyman skills that I had learned while with him certainly came into play—building the studded wall, painting and decorating and fitting out the kitchen. God is so good in training us for the future work that He has for us to do. Linda and I moved into the flat upstairs and at last had our own front door.

After renovating and converting the shop into a book shop, we contacted book wholesalers and began purchasing and selling books with a small startup budget, running the coffee shop alongside the book sales. I remember purchasing a coffee percolator, which I had never seen before, but I loved the fact that it filled the shop with the aroma of fresh ground coffee which, to me, was always appealing. We purchased Bibles and commentaries, books by old revivalists like Charles Finney, Hudson Taylor, Corrie Ten Boom, and more modern stories like Dennis Bennett's *Nine O'clock in the Morning*. We circulated leaflets to the churches in the town to let them know we had arrived and were there to serve the Christian community in Wigan. I also initiated bookstalls in three of the local churches and with the ministers I got to know over my years as a herald, persuaded them also to run book shops in their town, going as far afield as Halifax and allowing them a ten percent commission on what they sold. We also purchased ministry cassettes as well as popular Christian music records.

Within nine months, we were making sufficient profit for Pastor Ray to say, "The church is going to stop paying you now. You are going to be paid out of the earnings at the shop." One of the elders of the church was so surprised at this happening, he decided to give us £5 a week to supplement our income.

One of the most noticeable happenings in our new home was my realisation that my son had been born in sin and shaped in iniquity. The bad thoughts, actions and deeds that rested within Linda and I also could come forth in John. Many evenings just before going to bed, I would go into the darkness of this little room, sit on the floor with my feet under John's cot and tears would begin to flow as I prayed that God would graciously bring John to a knowledge of Himself. How I longed for my son to know Jesus. It would take me back to the moments of his birth. When the baby was first placed into Linda's arms in the delivery room, I put my arms under Linda's and we gave John to the Lord to be his servant. I have six lovely children. With each of them, we have dedicated them to the Lord as soon as they were placed in our arms at birth. I am so glad that the Lord has heard the cry of our heart as the six of them have come to faith and learned to serve the Lord Jesus. God has certainly been gracious to us to see our family serving God.

In early November of 1971, Pastor Ray came to the shop to tell us some sad news about two of the young boys who were attending our youth group, one 11 and the other 12-years-old. Their mother had died some four years earlier and they were living in one of the high-rise blocks of flats near the church. Both always appeared quiet and withdrawn. He said that because of their father's gambling habit, they were living in this cold flat with no heat or electric light. The last meal they had was cold pig's trotters and the Council was going to take them into care. He then said, "Do you think you and Linda may take them in?" It just so happened that I was about to pick Linda up from a visit she had made. She was heavily pregnant with our second son due in January 1972. I personally had just finished reading George Muller's book about opening an orphanage for fifty orphans and having no food for breakfast on the first day but God miraculously provided bread and soup at their door.

I sat in the car outside of our home and began to explain what was happening with Tony and Martin. As I concluded the story, I began to weep. Not knowing that we could claim anything from the local authority for their upkeep but having Muller's story so fresh in my mind, I said to Linda, "If Muller could believe God for fifty, could we not believe God for two?" And so, we entered a wonderful time of our lives, fostering these two young men.

One of them, Tony, went on to marry a minister's daughter and become a missionary in the Philippines caring for rejected babies who were born with hair lips and cleft palates. He then went on to not only build an orphanage but also a Bible college in Santiago City. He invited me many times to go and visit, but I have never wanted to travel. On the opening of their Bible college, he invited me to go again. Two friends were going and about ten days before they were due to set up, they came and said to me, "Pete, you must go. We have bought you the tickets."

At the grand opening, there were hundreds of people who had travelled from different communities to attend. What a wonderful experience to go and see the fantastic work that Tony had been able to complete. As the meeting started, he suddenly called me to the front. He put his arms around me, and I paraphrase his words, "Without this man's love and care for me, what you see around me today would never have happened." And then he said, "This is my real dad."

I don't think I can explain the emotions that flooded my being. I felt Linda and I had done so little; we had housed a boy in need, which Christ expects us to do. The Word of God in Luke 17:10 says, "When you have done all, you are only unprofitable servants." I felt so proud of this man who had achieved so much and would achieve so much more when he went to India and built more orphanages. Martin went on to become a headmaster of a senior school. Serving Jesus is just such a great privilege. I can never thank God enough for the blessing that I have seen in my life.

Let me tell you that while we were fostering these two boys, we received amazing provisions. Often, boxes of groceries would arrive on our stairs at the entrance to the shop. The husband of the first family we lived with worked at Heinz, and sometimes the labels would fall off the tins which Tom could purchase for a penny in the Heinz staff shop. Every week, we had a carrier bag full of Heinz tins which we never knew the contents of so opened them to have surprise meals. Sometimes beans, sometimes spaghetti, sometimes soup. The varieties were "57," but what a blessing. We had no money to buy games, so we invented them. One of them was to race on tins. We would use the tins and place them in a course around our living room. We then had to run on top of the tins and see who could run 'round the course the fastest without falling off.

Before leaving the story of our time in Wigan, let me tell you the amazing story of Bonsall Holiday Camp. Bonsall Holiday Camp was like going back into the nineteenth century. We had a tin hut, about twelve by eight feet, which was the kitchen with two domestic cookers in it. There was also the wooden Nissen hut, which was the dining hall, and another wooden Nissen hut, which was the meeting hall. We had a variety of accommodation: one was several bell tents that looked like they were surplus from the Boer War. The others were chalet tents which were basically hardboard structures with canvas roofs. The others were our chalets, which sound rather wonderful but were just garden sheds. Our toilets were chemical toilets, the buckets of which had to be emptied daily into a cesspit which was dug at the beginning of each season. But the blessing of God that rested on the eighty to one hundred children and young people who came there was phenomenal.

The first thing that Bob and Ray wanted to do was to build a new toilet block and showers. I became the labourer to help in the construction of that building. I was a man full of faith and on a mission, and when the first building blocks came out of the ground, it was my job to put building blocks around the site. It was 7 p.m. when those first building blocks protruded above the surface of the earth. The builders went home, and Ray went off to bed. I had this crazy notion that the God of heaven, who could do all things and passionately loved what we were doing to build His Kingdom, would be willing to help with the work during the night. So, the blocks that were required to build the structure began to move into place around the site.

Hour after hour, I toiled until I completed the task just after midnight. I then passionately cried out to the Lord, "Lord, You are the God of miracles. Please build this during the night while I sleep." I went off into the cabin that I was sharing with Ray. I climbed into bed and fell fast asleep.

At 6:30 a.m. the next morning, the sun was shining brightly. I hopped out of bed, pulled back the curtains and looked to see if the Almighty had finished the building during the night. To my surprise, the site remained as I had left it. The Almighty had not built it overnight. Ray then sat up in his bed and asked what I was doing. I told him what I had done and my prayer. He laughed and said, "You daft bat. God doesn't do things like that. He has given us the job of doing the practical work. He has left it in our hands to do the building." I still have that element of faith within me. If faith can move mountains, it just might be possible that faith could build buildings.

The other two things I had been given responsibility for at Wigan Church was to start a Silver Liners club for people over their sixties and to look after our youth work. Both of these I did with great relish. Our Silver Liners grew from zero to about sixty people whom I loved and had the responsibility to visit. I would take John with me, and of course, they were more interested in John than me, but we had lovely fellowship with them and saw many come to know the Lord. John would often come to that meeting with Linda and would fall asleep on the floor after running 'round and 'round. The youth work also grew, and we used to pick up a number of the kids in minibuses. We would have about fifty gather on a Friday evening. I had the privilege of teaching Ray's eldest daughter at the age of twelve years to play the guitar. Miriam was a superstar. My stay in Wigan was enjoyable, spiritually profitable, and a delight to our souls. Thank God for His goodness to us in the land of the living.

Chapter 8

Bramley consists mainly of three local authority housing estates in the metropolitan city of Leeds, a thriving hub
of commercial activity. It is on the Eastern side of the UK
and boasts many historical sites around its region. Wigan,
in contrast, was a working-class area where mills and coal
mines were its main industries, complying with the northern image of the working-class Industrial Revolution and
was based on the west side of the UK. I tell you this because
of the influence it had on the next stage of my journey in following Christ.

In 1973, I met the pastor of the Leeds AOG Church having also come into contact with his brother, David. The pastor from Leeds was an enthusiastic man, passionate about
serving God. He told me that they had opened a building about a dozen years earlier for the purpose of working
among children, young people and for Sunday school. So far
it had only progressed as a branch Sunday school and now
he was looking to pioneer a church in the building and asked
me to consider taking on the pastoral role. I was stirred in
my spirit about pioneering a church as my whole history in
ministry was about pioneering and winning people for Jesus.

As I prayed and sought the Lord, someone prophesied in the church that it was about time we moved on which, although it appeared to be generally for the church, certainly touched my heart.

The next week I was at the Holiday Centre at Bonsall getting ready for the season and spending some time alone. It gave me the opportunity to pray much more about the possibility of moving to Leeds. I thought I should seek advice from my former pastor, Norman Young, so I phoned him and discussed the opportunity that had arisen. He asked if I was still reading the Scriptures systematically as he had taught me. I replied yes and that it had become a habit in my daily life. He then replied, "Do you remember how I taught you that if you read the Scriptures systematically, God can speak to you from your daily readings?" This reminder prompted me to say to the Lord that evening, "Lord, please speak to me from Your Word."

Now let me tell you that I was reading through the early chapters of 1 Chronicles. If you know your Bible, you will know that this includes passages that tell of the history of the children of Israel and the anonymous characters who begat their children. It seemed an impossibility that God could speak to me from this particular chapter full of genealogies that I would be reading, but to my shock and amazement, it suddenly spoke of a family and when this person had begat his son, they moved to the east side of the country and found pasture. "Wow! Wow God, You are so amazing. I cannot believe that has just happened. Would You please do that again for me tomorrow, just to confirm that I need to move from the westside to the eastside of the country?" The next day I read the following chapter and my heart beat a little faster in the anticipation that God would do the same again. And He did! The family in the chapter moved to the east side and found good pasture for their flock. It was true. The Lord wanted me to pioneer a church in Bramley.

Please put up with me over the next few pages as I try to explain the complexities of that ministry which took place over the next four years. First of all, the church could only pay me £2 a week and had persuaded the local Council to offer us a three-bedroomed Council property on the nicest estate called the Snowden Estate. Our house was found on Snowden Avenue.

Because the income was so little, a member of the Leeds church called John, who worked for a life insurance company called Sun Life of Canada, had secured me a job working for them. I was grateful for this opportunity but dubious about selling life insurance. This was until I discovered that the company I would be working for was one of only three companies in the country that worked on having guaranteed valuations in their policies. This ensured the client had a policy that had a written valuation after the first two years of investment until the final year when that policy matured.

The second thing was the startup congregation. It was made up of an elderly couple, the wife running the Sunday school who would come to the church with her husband, and also a mother who had two illegitimate children, one a 12-year-old son who was mad on rugby and a 14-year-old daughter. Our first Sunday service consisted of Gladys and George, Irene and June, Linda, myself and my two small children, Simon and John. Gladys knew how to play about a dozen hymns, and so, with these folks we commenced the ministry. From that moment, I was amazed at how the work grew. I am sure it was nothing to do with me but that the sovereign hand of God was amongst us.

I was now working full-time selling life insurance. In the summer, I had committed myself to working with Ray Belfield in the Holiday Centre, primarily working with youth and children. The rest of the time I was working to build the church. We opened a youth ministry during the week, broke bread on Sunday morning, preached the Gospel on Sunday evening and on Saturday afternoon, I went to the town centre, stood on the chair I took with me and held an open-air meeting. The spot was approximately 600 meters from the church building. I became quite successful at selling life insurance, and within eighteen months, I was able to validate my income by only working one day a week and earning five days' wages in one day. The youth work began to grow and thrive until we had thirty to forty young people coming regularly. After nine months, I was able to save enough money to put a deposit on a new detached Barratts property just about 250 meters from the church.

We had another elderly couple and another family join us and then we had Mrs. Heaton, who was a real pianist, also join us. Our new pianist had terrible eyesight and virtually had her nose on the sheet music to be able to play the hymns, but despite this, she played remarkably well. Her elderly friend joined and then another family, and so we continued to grow. During the course of these families coming, people came and gave their lives to Jesus. A young Asian man was brought by one of the families, and he gave his life to Christ. A young Polish man, called Victor, was brought by one of the families and gave his life to Christ. Three or four people came to know the Lord from the open-air meetings as well. One was Angela, a lovely young woman of eighteen years of age.

After moving into our newly acquired home, I decided to build an extension and a garage on the property. This helped us accommodate some young men who needed help. One young man was an Irish Nigerian Jew who came to know Christ at Bonsall and came back year after year since the age of thirteen. Now at the age of eighteen, he said that God had told him to come and work with me, and so he became our first lodger in the new house in Eightlands Lane. Then my brother phoned me from Walthamstow to ask if Linda and I could take in a young Muslim boy of sixteen who had come to know Christ and had been thrown out of the family home without anywhere to live. As you are aware, God had already given us compassionate hearts, so after just turning seventeen, this young man arrived to become our second lodger. Then I had a call from Ray Belfield about a young university postgraduate who hadn't been able to take the strain of university life and had become an alcoholic. They had not been able to do anything to help him, and as I was the patron saint of hopeless causes, he asked if we could take him in. Thank God for the extension. Yes, we would take him. Then one of the boys we had fostered had won a place at Leeds University and he asked if he could come and live with us and so our fourth lodger arrived. These four all grew in God and came together as a remarkable team to build the church even more.

At the same time, Ray decided that he would sell the Holiday Centre since his partner Bob was moving to take on a pastorate in Australia. I believed that God did not want this Holiday Centre to leave the Kingdom of Heaven, so I pleaded with him to sell it to me. Although I did not have a penny in my pocket to purchase it, I believed that God would help us fund it, and so he agreed to sell it to me for £12,000, which I would need to repay over the next five years.

How amazing is the hand of God when we live by faith? Holding down a job, looking after four young men, caring for a young family, Linda being pregnant with our third child, building a church and now building up a new Holiday Centre; this was truly the amazing purpose of God in the land of the living.

Let me tell you of a wonderful experience that took place in the life of the church. I had become friends with a number of ministers around us in the local area. I have always believed that we are One Body and that churches are not there to compete with one another but to complement one another. One church decided to have a crusade and invited a well-known evangelist to come. It was really successful and about thirty or forty people came to know Christ, but this friend of mine found that working with the evangelist was really exhausting. The evangelist always insisted, after a week's crusade, on coming back for a weekend three months later. My friend thought he could not cope with the hectic schedule that he would have to follow and virtually pleaded with me to have the evangelist preach at our church for the weekend. I readily agreed and prepared. Having received the leaflets to advertise the coming event, I distributed them around the local area.

On the Friday prior to the first meeting on the Saturday, there was a knock on my door. A tall, gaunt man, about sixty years of age, stood there holding one of the leaflets. He asked if he could speak to me. I invited him in, and he seated himself in one of the armchairs next to the fire. On the leaflet, it announced that the Gospel would be preached and the sick would be healed. He handed me the leaflet and said, "Do you really believe this?" In my lifetime, I had never been put in a position of expressing my faith that God would heal the sick in such a way. My reply was, "I believe it." He said to me, "I have lung cancer. I have been given three months to live. Do you believe God can heal me?"

I wonder how many of you reading this book have been put in that position. I would say that it is certainly challenging. A man dying with lung cancer sits in front of you and asks you if God can heal him. My verbal answer was, "Yes, I believe God can heal you." But in my head, I was like the man in the Scriptures, "Lord, help thou, my unbelief." The weekend flew past. We had two other people come to Christ, and the man who visited me, a bus inspector, was duly prayed for by the evangelist who readily declared that he was healed. But then again, the evangelist was leaving the next day and would not have to bear the consequence if he was not healed.

On Monday, the man went to the hospital for his normal checkup, and around 6 p.m., he knocked on my door again. He was smiling and asked, "Can I come in and talk to you?" He came in, sat in the same armchair by the fire and said, "You won't believe it." I asked, "I won't believe what?" He said, "I went to the hospital for my normal checkup. They took the X-ray and then the consultant called me in, put it on the screen and said, 'There is something wrong here, we need to take another one.' They then took a second X-ray and I returned again to see the consultant. He said to me, 'Mr. Clay, I am totally mystified by these X-rays. I don't know what has happened, but there is no sign of any cancer in your lungs.' The consultant said, 'I am completely blank regarding this issue, but all I can tell you is you are completely free from cancer.'"

You can imagine how I felt. I wanted to whoop for joy. I wanted to jump up and down on the sofa. If I could have, I would have turned cartwheels, but Arnold Clay was a very dignified man, so I kept my excitement down and said, "Arnold, that is really wonderful." Arnold and his wife, our first dignified professional couple, became faithful members of the Bramley Church. We were really becoming a great representation of the different folk in those three estates.

We saw a number of people healed during my time at

the church, but I must tell you of one other instance. Angela Cobbold was a very pretty girl of fifteen. She came to know Christ in our youth work and came regularly Sunday morning and evening to the services. One Sunday morning, her father unexpectedly turned up to the service. He seemed to enjoy the singing, the breaking of bread and the ministry of God's Word. He wore a flat cap that he continued to wear all through the service.

As he was leaving, I spoke to him at the door and said how nice it was that he had visited with us. I asked why he had come that particular morning. He said, "I came to be prayed for because my daughter has been telling me about people who have been healed when they come to church. The reason I am wearing my cap is that I have had a large growth on my head which the surgeons have told me was inoperable and it keeps growing. So, I came here this morning for you to pray for it." My question then was, "Why didn't you come forward and let us pray for it?" He then took his hat off and there was no sign of any large growth on his head. He then said to me, "I don't know what happened, but it disappeared while I sat in the church." How amazing and good the dear Almighty is when the Church is full of faith. For I am sure it was the faith of the people that healed the man that day.

Let me tell you of just one more healing. The estates that made up our area started at the poshest, the Snowdens, then moved down to the Rayvilles, and at the bottom were the Houghleys where most of the unemployed lived. The Houghleys were properties built in the 1930s with huge gardens, most of them overgrown with bushes and weeds, often with old prams, bike tires, and bedsteads hidden among the brambles. Some of our young people came from this estate and two of them told us of their mother's heart condition.

Now with all our youth, we would visit their homes and get to know the family, and this particular family lived in poor conditions. The carpet looked like it hadn't been cleaned for the last hundred years and the sofa was so threadbare that the springs were about to pop out. On visiting that family, you did it with a prayer as they would offer you tea in a mug that appeared not to have been washed for the last month. One didn't look into the mug but, by the grace of God, sipped the tea believing that the Almighty would give you immunity over any unwelcome guests that might be found in it. We prayed that the heart condition of this lady would go and then we left the home. The following Sunday, the mum, dad, and the five kids all arrived in church. All gave their lives to Christ and thanked the Lord for the healing of their mother, for she had gone to hospital that week and the heart murmur was completely gone.

Chapter 9

Although there are many other stories we could write about Bramley, I do want to tell you about the Holiday Centre that we purchased and the fantastic ministry that took place on that wonderful hillside adjacent to the Peak National Park.

As previously mentioned, Bonsall Camp in many ways was like moving back to the late nineteenth or early twentieth century in its layout and style. The entrance to the campsite was situated on the top right-hand corner of the field, past a cowshed and onto a flatter piece of ground that led down a steep hill to where the dining hall, kitchen, and meeting hall were located. The washing facilities were two large drums of reasonably hot water placed outside the kitchen. From here, staff and guests used plastic bowls to scoop out the water which they then used to wash themselves in their accommodation. This water was also used by kitchen staff to wash the dishes, etc. in a tin bath on a table. The view from the field is absolutely outstanding. One could not wish for a more tranquil and beautiful site for the camp to be situated at.

Now God had laid upon my heart to build a completely new brick complex and to replace the chalets with reasonably modern caravans. From the very beginning of this project, the hand of God was with us. Many of the events that I will tell you of, I really do not know how they happened or where the money came from to bring the provision we needed at certain moments in time. All I can say is that for the next five to six years while building, the hand of God was with us.

Firstly, we needed an architect to create the building and to have the plans passed by the local authority. As we were on the edge of Peak National Park, having the need of an architect was essential, and God amazingly brought us into contact with a young man in Bramley who had just set up his practice. For some unknown reason, he took to us, and having explained what the project was and how it would benefit needy children and young people, he offered to design the building, put together the proposal of how it could be constructed, and handle the local authority. So, the plans that he had drawn went off to the local Council, and to our amazement, they loved them and were passed.

In April of that year, we commenced work on constructing the first building, which would be the kitchen and the storehouse with some bedroom space for staff as well. As I have already mentioned, during our time in Bramley, we had four young men who lived with us and so, with their help, the first task was to dig the foundations. Bright and early one morning late in April, having purchased a hundred-foot tape, one of the young men and I measured out the outline of that first building at the bottom of the field.

On a Friday night, three of the young men and myself

travelled to the site, and on Saturday morning, with picks and shovels, we began to dig the foundation of the kitchen. Let me say, I was totally surprised at the size of the building which was forty feet long and twenty-five feet wide; that is about the size of two bungalows! As the young man I had taken to measure the site had the end that told us when we would get to forty feet, I felt I was climbing the hill forever before he told me to stop. We dug all day and threw the soil into the centre of what would be the new building. We came down to a rock called tufa stone which is a stone that is like honeycomb.

As we were down to a stone base, we thought this would be acceptable for the building inspector to pour a concrete foundation onto. So, I asked for the building inspector to come and look at our foundation. When he visited, he said that the foundation was excellent, but we would need to go down another six inches into the tufa stone. "By the way," he added, "you will need to take off all the soil you have thrown into the middle, and also all the grass that is underneath must be removed for the laying of the concrete." We duly laboured on, had the foundations passed by the building inspector, mixed the concrete and poured it, and by the time the camp commenced in July, we were ready to start laying the concrete blocks which would be the foundation of this new construction.

The camp went extremely well that year; many youngsters and teenagers came to Christ, many were filled with the Holy Ghost, and many felt the call of God on their lives. Week after week, the ministry was superb.

One of the families that came that year came from a village called Ryhope on the northeastern coast of England. The man happened to be a builder by trade, the very thing we were lacking. He was enthused by what we were seeking to achieve and offered his services to do the bricklaying and plastering if we supplied the labour to bring the blocks and mix the mortar, ready for him to do the job. In the second week of August, we commenced the laying of the blocks. Week by week, we saw the progress: up to the window level, putting the windows in and then up to putting the roof plate on. Now we needed someone who could help us construct the roof.

When I had arrived at Wigan Church, the building was still being built, and I met a young man called Vernon Cowler who was working on the internal staircase. I talked to him about Christ, and he wonderfully became a Christian. He later married one of the young people who came to our youth work called Veronica, and they had two wonderful daughters born to them. Vernon, now a fully qualified joiner, volunteered to make the roof trusses with the secondhand timber we purchased. When they were made, they duly arrived at the campsite early in October, as we were trying to get the tiles on the roof before winter came. I was amazed that he and his wife were able to pull these roof trusses into place and nail them down.

In Bramley, we had come across a builder who also had fallen in love with us and was helping us build an extension on the church. The builder, Staveley, said that his original job was putting tiles on roofs, and he was happy to come and put them on the roof at Bonsall. So, in mid-October, the roof was completed and now the building was waterproof.

Then something very amazing happened. A man passing through Bonsall village popped in to see the building. Now if you recall, we had been cooking on domestic cookers and we needed industrial cookers which we had no hope of financing as our coffers were already virtually empty. This man just came and walked into what was really still a building site because there was no plaster on the wall or ceiling, the electrics were at their first fix stage and there was still rubble over the concrete floor. To my amazement, he lifted his hands heavenward and said, "God is in this place. I will buy you two industrial cookers." You can imagine how my heart leapt. This was the first of many, shall we say, miraculous happenings as we continued to build for the glory of God.

Now let us just pause a moment and think what has happened in the last six months: an architect came on board from nowhere, three labourers were living in my own house, the Council gave planning permission, a builder arrived and said he would build for free, a carpenter said he would build roof trusses for free, a roofer said he would put our roof on for free and now we had two industrial cookers bought for us for free. I almost forgot an electrician arrived and said he would do the wiring for free. Surely, this must be God working with us.

The next jobs were to build the store cupboards, build the bedroom, fit the kitchen, tile the walls, put plasterboard on the ceiling, plaster, and get the plumbing in, all this being made ready for the following year and the grand opening of our new kitchen facilities. One of the local churches in Nottingham who had attended camp that year had a plumber in their church who volunteered to come and do the plumbing when we were ready. It so happened that during the winter, a number of things transpired that were so helpful to us.

A Holiday Centre in Matlock was going to be pulled down and turned into flats. I visited the demolition contractor and asked them what they were going to do with the kitchen. He said they would just throw it away. "Could we have it?" I asked. "You take it out, and you can have it," he replied. So, the stainless steel double drainer sinks with kitchen cabinets and surfaces and all the things we needed were duly removed from the demolition site and installed in the new kitchen at Bonsall Camp. They looked fabulous. Amazingly, we were told of an auction where some of the lots going under the hammer were stock from a tile company going bankrupt. We purchased all the tiles we needed for £10. Wow! We then purchased the plasterboards, electric sockets, and wiring, and later tiled the floor and walls and had the industrial cookers installed.

By the time the following summer came, we were about ready to feed the "five thousand." It seemed that at every turn, the sunshine of the Almighty was shining on us. So, our second season also began with the blessing of God resting upon us. Many kids and young people again came to faith or were filled with the Holy Ghost and called into ministry.

At the end of the season, we began digging the foundations of the second building which would be the new dining hall. Our first job was to demolish the old timber building, and we reclaimed all the timber from that building to help us with the new construction. By late October, we had the foundations completed, the concrete poured and commenced laying the first concrete blocks. We had two requirements to help us forward the construction. One was 400 tons of stone to fill the foundation as the building being erected was on the slope of the hill and the ground needed leveling up. By mid-November, the need for that stone for the foundation had become a critical issue and our coffers were totally empty.

One morning, I was driving into Cromford to buy provisions for that weekend to keep us fed and supply us with hot tea as the weather had turned bitterly cold and we were lighting fires in the foundations to give us some warmth. At the bottom of Clatterway as you left the village stood a pub called the Pig of Lead. Part of its car park was an old quarry, and for some unknown reason, the brewery had decided to extend the parking facilities and was blasting stone from the quarry face for that improvement.

As I drove past, the Spirit of the Lord spoke to me and said, "Go into the car park and ask them what they are doing with that stone." As usual, I argued with the Almighty. "Lord, You don't just stop your vehicle and go ask people what they are doing with their stone." So, I continued to drive down Via Gellia to Cromford. The Lord continued to prompt me, "Go and ask what they are doing with the stone." I continued to say, "No, Lord, that is silly. People don't do that."

By the time I was entering the next village, the pressure had mounted on me and I thought I would get no peace unless I went and asked. So, I drove back to the Pig of Lead, drove into the car park, spoke to one of the labourers and asked if I could speak to the foreman. A really big chap, about six foot two, with broad shoulders and well made, came out. "What can I do for you?" I asked, "What are you doing with this stone?" He didn't say a word, he just picked up a large sledge-hammer, walked over to a reasonably sized piece of rock, lifted the hammer, hit the rock and the hammer bounced up. He said, "This is one of the hardest volcanic rocks known to man. We have to drive seven miles to tip it as it is of little use to anyone." My comment to him was, "Would you like to tip it a little closer?" I said, "Follow me."

The campsite was about three quarters of a mile from the quarry face. He was delighted to have somewhere to tip his waste stone and we were delighted to receive it. Load after load arrived in twenty-ton vehicles to the top of the field. The next problem we had was transporting the stone from the top of the field to our building site some hundred meters away. All that we had was a hand-pushed barrow, so load after load, we toiled at moving the stone from the top of the field to the bottom. We thanked God that at least we were pushing it downhill and not up, and we thanked God that we eventually had sufficient stone to fill the hole. We had bought a small concrete mixer and had already purchased the sand, stone and cement to mix the concrete to lay the floor. By the end of January, we had completed the work and were moving up to the window level. That was our next problem. We needed twenty windows, all four foot square, and as I have already said, there was no money left in the bank. What would we do?

That month, I heard there was an auction that was taking place where some of the auction lots were building materials that were surplus to requirement. On my arrival and to my amazement, there were 20 four foot square wooden window frames. I could not believe my eyes. In modern terms, we are talking of £3,000 worth of windows and I only had £2 in my pocket. I talked to the Lord, "Lord, You know we need these windows, and You know the cost and You know we can't afford to buy them. Please give us favour at this auction and let us buy them."

Lot after lot went under the auctioneer's hammer until the window frames were called. I said to the Lord, "I am going to make the first bid and I'll bid what we have, and you know that is all we have." So, I made the opening bid, my heart was in my mouth and it seemed an eternity passed as the auctioneer asked for any other bids. All was silent and he said, "If not, I will take this bid. Going for the first time, going for the second time. Sold to the gentleman on my right." We had acquired the windows we needed for £2! I couldn't believe my ears when the auctioneer said, "Sold to the gentleman on my right." I don't know if you call the provision of the stone and the windows miracles, but certainly, the hand of God seemed to be helping us every step of the way.

Come the summer, we had the building up, the roof on and the windows in. We had built the pillars to put the steel girders on to support the joists on which the upper floor would be laid. Vernon, our carpenter, made the staircase to go in the corner of the building, and the doors for the fire exits were put on. So, we now had a huge open space upstairs and a new dining room. But there was still more to do as there was no plaster on the wall, plasterboards on the ceiling, or bedrooms completed on the upper floor. At least we could use downstairs as the dining room.

The bookings that year were very good, and it meant we had money in the kitty to continue the work in the autumn. The downside was we did not have enough space to put the staff, so we carried mattresses upstairs, laid them on the floor in the large empty space, and as there were more female staff than male, we allowed the ten ladies to sleep upstairs. Sadly, the building inspector came 'round, inspected both buildings and said that they were perfect, but it was illegal to sleep people upstairs, so we had to move them immediately. When he left, I sat on the stairs and just cried. I said, "Oh God, we are working hard. Where are we going to put these people to sleep now?" By God's grace, we were able to shuffle people 'round and squeeze them into odd corners all over the camp. We had a wonderful season with boys and girls coming to faith, people being baptized in the Holy Ghost, and people feeling the call of God on their lives. God was always so gracious to us in seeing so many young lives changed.

Year after year, a children's evangelist called Dave Lakin

came and brought his unique brand of ministry, which touched the hearts of so many. Dave was just a superstar. Anyone who has been to Bonsall and heard Dave will know how precious he was and how, week after week, all the kids went on his famous Lion Hunt. If none of you have been on Dave Lakin's Lion Hunt, you have missed an absolute treat. I wished I could really explain it to you, so forgive me now if I ramble on a little to try and give you the picture of this exciting event.

Dave would commence the event with these words to the children, "We're going on a Lion Hunt. All you have to do is say what I say." Then he would say, "We're going on a Lion Hunt," and the kids would repeat, "We're going on a Lion Hunt." Then he would say, "Where's me gun?" and they would say, "Where's me gun?" Then he would say, "Where's me wellies?" and the kids would repeat what he was saying. He would say such things as "here's a swamp"—all this was in the meeting room with the kids sitting there—and they would say, "Here's a swamp." He would hold his nose and say, "It's a smelly swamp." The kids would copy him and then he would say, "Stinky poo."

The kids just loved saying what he was saying, and they were with him on this adventure until they came to the place where he would say, "We've found a lion—shsssssh," and then he would say, "Where's me gun? Here's me gun. Take aim . . . bang! We've killed a lion. Hurray!"

Then he would say, "That's it," and the kids would say, "That's it."

Dave would say, "No! It's the end of the Lion Hunt," and they would say, "No! It's the end of the Lion Hunt."

"No!" he would shout. "It's the end of the Lion Hunt," and they would repeat, "No! It's the end of the Lion Hunt."

He would say, "No! It's really finished." They would say, "No! It's really finished," and then he would say, "Oh, shut up," and they would say, "Oh, shut up."

Then he would say, "You're daft," and they would shout back, "You're daft," and then he would say, "Who's daft?" and every time he got the same response, "You're daft," in a mass of kids voices and they would all collapse in a heap of laughter.

Dave Lakin's Lion Hunts were unique in the annals of Bonsall's history. Dave Lakin is one of the unsung heroes of ministry in the AOG. I would say thousands of children and young people had their lives changed because of the unique ministry of this wonderful man and I wish to honour him for all the great works he completed.

Another great thing that Dave introduced to Bonsall was the Friday afternoon humongous water fight. We would have a sports afternoon and when it had finished someone would throw water over someone else. Who it was that threw the water I can never remember, but soon the field was full of kids, party leaders, staff and the ministry team running 'round with buckets and bowls full of water and soaking everybody in sight. It was always one of the great fun afternoons. No one was missed; all were soaked and the howls of laughter were heard in every corner of the campsite.

Many of the kids when they left on the Saturday morning cried as they didn't want to leave this happy place where the Spirit of God truly rested. Thanks to Dave, it was certainly a place of joy, of laughter, and of spiritual well-being.

Mr. Lakin, I salute you.

Chapter 10

Let us move on to the building of the meeting hall which was to be attached to the dining hall. We had engaged a builder to help us progress the work on the new meeting hall and he had brought it up to ground level. This meant as we were building on the hill that we needed to purchase 200 tons of stone to make the ground floor level. As before, we had spent up and had very little in the kitty. In fact, we had enough to purchase between five to ten tons of stone.

On the final Sunday of the final week of camp in the morning, I got all the staff into the kitchen. It was turning out to be one of those beautiful hot summer days, and I said to them, "Guys, we need to pray for a miracle for either the funds to come in or someone to donate stone to us because if we are to be ready for next summer, we need to fill that 200-ton hole." So, all of us prayed fervently that God would help us to fill the hole.

During the afternoon, about two o'clock, a man walked onto the field, came up to me and said, "I understand that you are looking for stone." I confirmed that we were. Ben Bennett, one of the larger quarries in the area, had made too much "crusher run" which was the stone we needed to fill the hole. Ben Bennett was selling it off at £15 per load. I thanked him for the information, knowing the most we could carry was 1,500 pounds of weight in a small van, which again meant our funds could not purchase very much. I pondered in my own thinking, "Who has told this chap that we need stone? For no one has been into the village to inform people of our need."

Then another amazing event occurred. About 4 p.m., having five minutes of rest in the sunshine, another man arrived on the field. He said, "I understand you need stone delivering." How did this chap know that we wanted stone? I replied that we would love to have stone delivered. He said, "I am working here for the next five days and I will be driving my wagon into the village and it will be empty every evening for the next five working days." I asked, "How much stone can your vehicle carry?" He said, "Twenty tons." I almost squealed with pleasure. This guy could bring twenty tons in, but how much would that cost? He gave us a price and I quickly calculated that we could afford to buy 100 tons, which was still short of the 200 tons required.

Now this is where my daft faith springs into life. I said in my heart to the Lord, "Lord, did you send an angel into the village to tell these people of our need? I believe you must have done because no one from the campsite has been down to tell of our need. Therefore, You know we can only afford to buy 100 tons, so I am going to believe You that if I order 100 tons of stone, You are the God who is able to fill the 200-ton hole with 100 tons of stone." So, I said to the man with the lorry, "Bring us five loads, one each night that you are coming into the village." So, every evening the man arrived with his cargo of twenty tons of stone. Every evening we raked the stone out and I walked around the inside of that hole saying, "God, I believe that you are going to fill this 200-ton hole with 100 tons of stone."

Our God never fails. Come Friday night when we had raked the last twenty tons of stone, the floor was completely level. Either there is a gap under that stone on which it must float, or God created an additional 100 tons of stone. What an amazing God we serve! It meant that we could now borrow from the bank on the property that we had built and by the time the next summer season arrived, we had completed the dining room, the bedrooms upstairs, the meeting hall and the bedrooms above. We had put new toilet facilities in the main building, and we had a fabulous new building to serve the children and young people that would come year on year.

Just to top this off, in the eighth year, I had moved to Bishop Auckland to pastor a church there, and the industrial cooker that had been purchased during our first year of building had worn out, so we were in desperate need of two new cookers. We had saved some money, a very little amount of money, to purchase my wife a new washing machine at an auction in Darlington and so, on a Thursday morning, I travelled to Darlington. Now in today's money, these two industrial cookers were going to cost us in the region of £4,000, and the money I had to spend on the secondhand washing machine was about £100. I had a small Mini Traveller as my mode of transport, and so I set off to Darlington to purchase the washing machine.

I arrived at the auction, and as I walked towards the building, in the yard outside, there were two brand spanking new industrial cookers, still wrapped in their corrugated cardboard, unopened. You can imagine my amazement at seeing them in the auction yard, knowing how we so desperately needed these cookers for the camp.

I looked for the lot number, but there was none to be found. The auctioneer knew me by face, because on several occasions in the last year I had purchased items. So, I approached him and asked, "Are these cookers in the auction today?" He replied, "Yes, they are." I said, "They have no number on them." He came and looked and said, "You are right. There is no number on them." Then he said, "Are you interested? They have come out of the VAT office in Harrogate which has now closed down and they haven't come out of their wrapping to be installed." My reply was, "I am interested." So, he then asked, "Being there is no number on them, do you want to make me an offer?" I just had this £100 in my pocket which I thought was no way enough to buy them, but it was all I had. So, I asked, "Would you take £100?" He looked at me and spoke. "Go on, you can have them for your cheek." I got two of his men to help me push one of them into the back of my Mini Traveller. It weighed the back down so much that it looked like I was about to take off for the moon.

I drove back to Bishop Auckland, and my kids met me on the drive. "Have you got mum's new washing machine?" I had to confess, "No, I haven't, but I have got two industrial cookers for the Holiday Camp." God is just so wonderful in making provisions. Within a fortnight, one of the folks in the church gifted us a really good washing machine that was of no further use to them. In so many ways, we see the gift of God working in our lives. Those cookers were then delivered to the Holiday Camp and duly installed. What a blessing they were to us, and for the next fifteen years, they gave faithful service and enabled us to cook thousands of meals for all those that came to Bonsall Adventure Camp.

During the seven years of building the camp, Bramley Church grew, and we needed to extend the building. Four of the young men who came to Christ went into the ministry: one as a youth leader in Wakefield, another went to Mattersey Bible College, the third pioneered a church in Rugby, and the fourth went to be a youth worker in Ulverston. We bought ourselves an old minibus, and then I decided that we would need a coach. So again, off to the auction I went. This time I had in my pocket the equivalent of £1,000 and there were a number of coaches and buses that were going through the auction on that day. I remember fixing my eyes on a brown, single-decker, fifty-two seater coach, and the bidding began. I knew this vehicle was worth about £5,000 and so didn't think we had a chance of buying it.

The bids went up in today's money in increments of £100, so I bid £200, then £400, then £600, and then £800.

The person bidding against me bid £900, and I said to the Lord, "Well, Lord, I can only go to £1,000, so if you want us to have it, I need to get it at £1,000." Once again, the Lord was with us, and we purchased our own coach for £1,000. Over the next fifteen months, we saw many adventures in taking our coach on Saturday day trips, quite often filling the fifty-two seats. God truly blessed us in our ministry within the Bramley Church, and I thank God for every soul that came to know Jesus during that time of ministry.

During this time, I was invited to be the guest speaker at the AOG, Bishop Auckland Church. Now Bishop Auckland was one of our historic churches, well known throughout our fellowship. It was started in the 1930s when a crusade was held by the brothers, Steven and George Jeffries. The remarkable story of its commencement is worth telling now.

I believe there were between six and ten people who began to pray together that God would revive Bishop Auckland in the County of Durham, which had a population of approximately 10,000. Then they felt that God led them to invite Steven and George Jeffries to come and have an evangelistic crusade in the town. They hired the town hall on the town square by which the main street ran, which would have been about three quarters of a mile in length. When they arrived, their advertisement was a blackboard leaning against a chair which announced: 'Gospel service to be held here at 6:30 p.m. every evening. The sick will be prayed for.' For the first three or four days, approximately ten to a dozen people attended the meetings.

There was a girl in the town, aged about 12-years-old at the time, who tapped her way down the High Street every weekday to attend the school that was situated on the town square. On the fourth or fifth day, she arrived at the town hall with her parents to be prayed for. Now this was recounted to me by a member of the Bishop Auckland Church who knew the girl personally. After the Gospel had been preached, the girl was brought to the front for the hands of the evangelist to be laid on her. Just like Bartimaeus, the parents said to the evangelist, "We would love our daughter to receive her sight." The evangelist put his hands on her eyes and looking heavenward prayed that God would be merciful and touch this girl's eyes and give her sight. To the amazement of those in the congregation, or should I say astonishment of those present, the girl's eye sockets, which had been empty from her birth, filled with two beautiful eyes. I hope we all can imagine how the town reacted when this girl who had tapped her way down the High Street for the last six years with her white cane can now walk the high street with two beautiful new blue eyes.

Before the end of the week, they were queuing six deep to get into the town hall, and many more of the inhabitants of Bishop Auckland were touched by the Gospel and by the healing hand of the Almighty. When the evangelist left, over 2,500 people had come to know Christ. How amazing that twenty-five percent of the town had given their lives to Jesus. The upshot was that the AOG took up temporary accommodation in the town hall and soon purchased an old factory on Railway Street for a congregation of 500 people attending worship every Sunday. So, this is the town I travelled to fulfill the commitment of preaching at their 50th anniversary celebration.

At that time, unbeknown to me, they did not have a minister. The church was perhaps a sad reflection of its revival days having now only about seventy in the congregation. Within four weeks of my visit, I had an invitation to be interviewed by the elders of the church in respect to becoming the pastor of this historic AOG church. While I had been at their anniversary service, I had been strangely moved with compassion towards the people that attended, particularly the younger group of men and women in their twenties of which there were about eighteen to twenty-five. All had been brought up in the church and now seemed to have a passion to serve God which motivated my feelings towards them as one thing the Lord has continually laid on my heart is to see young men and women coming into the ministry. Jesus said to His disciples, "'The harvest is great, but the labourers are few. Pray that the Lord of the harvest will bring labourers into the harvest field.'" By the grace of God, I could see a number of these men and women being fit for ministry, and my heart began to ache for them and for the town of Bishop Auckland. Therefore, when they asked me to go, I felt the Lord stirring in my spirit to move from Bramley to Bishop Auckland.

Chapter 11

Pride is a strange bedfellow. It creeps up on us unexpectedly and so it did with me at this moment in my life. I had
been in the ministry for just seven years and now had been
invited to pastor one of our movement's historic churches.
This was a very prestigious role. The church would not only
pay me a full-time wage that was a third more than I was
earning, but it also had a lovely manse, which came free of
charge. So, there was no mortgage to pay, and on top of that,
I got a car allowance. My, I had really arrived!

The elderly couple that had housed me when I had
gone to speak at the convention was just lovely, and I got on
really well with them. Of course, when visiting them, they
addressed me as Peter, but now that I was the pastor of their
church, when they addressed me as Peter, I corrected them;
I was now Pastor Peter Cunningham. It makes me cringe
when I think of my arrogance at that moment in my life.
All that I had and am—the lovely family that I had around
me, a faithful wife, three lovely children and a fourth on the
way, the growth in the ministry at Bramley and at Bonsall,
the success that I had in the job that had been allocated to
me in Leeds—all these were down to the good hand of God,

and nothing to do with my own talent and abilities, because truly any talent that we have is never ours; it is God-given. So please, let us be thankful every day of our lives that God gives us the ability and the privilege of serving Him.

How gracious was God over the next two years! Bonsall continued to grow and develop, the church at Bishop Auckland began to grow, and within eighteen months we had gone from 70 folks to 150. So full were we on a Sunday night that people were turned away as we did not have enough space to accommodate them. I was now not only leading a historic church but a church that had six elders, five of which were at a simmering war with one another. Families were feuding with one another under the surface. I had not been in this situation before and just did not know how to handle it. My passion was to see people coming to Christ. Two of the husbands of the young families to whom I related well were now assistant pastors with me and two more were prospective assistant pastors. Eventually, the first two were invited to take on churches and become evangelists, a third was invited to become an assistant minister, and the fourth went off to a nearby town to set up a new church.

This was one of the things God called and instructed me to do within that church structure—to take on some of these young families and train them for the ministry and then launch them into their own full-time ministry. One of them rose to be the superintendent of that region. So, in that sense, I fulfilled the purpose of God in that area of ministry. The others I believed were to take the church into larger premises. A school became vacant in the town centre. I paid an architect myself to draw up plans to convert the school into a community centre, not just a church hall but a place to accommodate and minister to all manner of needs that the town had. It would also provide accommodation for training young men and women for ministry as well as provide two flats for missionaries when they were home on furlough. We had sufficient funds to purchase this property. It had a large playground at the back of the building and fields beyond that. It was ideal for all the purposes I envisaged in God that this church could be involved in. I also considered two houses that were derelict that could be turned into accommodation for the homeless and a shop on the town's High Street to open as a coffee bar and book shop.

All these strategies I took to the elders. They viewed the school, they viewed the houses, and they viewed the shop. They hummed and hawed, they disagreed with one another, and they prevaricated and procrastinated. On and on this went, and eventually, the school was sold to a supermarket. Unbeknown to us, the County Council's Highway Department was planning a ring road to bypass the town square and to bring the main road through to the top of the town. This meant they needed to purchase the majority of the playground for a dual carriageway. When this did take place, it meant that the supermarket got all the money back that it had paid for its purchase. I now look at this and think, "God knows the future." If we had bought that school, it would have been completely paid for by the County Council's purchase of the playground for the purpose of the ring road they were planning.

By the time I had been there eighteen months, not only was the school sold but also the two derelict houses with a large piece of land behind that could have been turned into allotments to train the homeless people who would have been housed there. We had an ideal man in the church who certainly would have relished helping with these projects, but the shop was sold and all three areas of vision were now closed.

For the next six months, I felt as though I was wandering in no man's land, frustrated with myself in the arrogance that I had shown, saying sorry to the Lord for my attitude and actions and frustrated that I could take the church no further. The youth work and the children's work had grown. The Silver Liners, a group for the elderly, had been instituted and grown. A tank that they had built for a baptistry which had remained in the church's backyard for ten years was installed in the church, and we baptized several people. The Sunday night service had grown to capacity. In addition, I was dealing with six men who could not agree with one another and looked like they would never agree with one another as a millennium passed. I concluded at the end of that two years that God had made an investment in me and that investment was just not paying its way, so perhaps it was time to move on.

With sadness in my heart, I went to the next elders meeting with a letter of resignation and explained to the guys that I just could not remain there. All of them showed sadness at my decision, and some of them were reluctant to accept my resignation but, in my heart of hearts, I felt I could go no further with this group of people, and I would look to the Lord for my next step. This came surprisingly quickly and really out of the blue.

The minister of the Wigan church, where I had done my training, had decided to take his family on a world tour for a year. His wife was a talented singer, his daughter and his son were both talented like their mother and, therefore, as a family, they were well equipped to do a world tour. I had a phone call asking if I could come and look after the church for a year and be the senior leader. As I felt I needed time to readjust to knowing what the will of God was in my life, I agreed to take up that position and see where it would lead. So now, Linda, myself and our four children packed up our bags and moved down to Wigan.

This next part of my life I would like to come back to later in another book. There are many more things that happened that were quite extraordinary and in the will of God in the years that lay ahead. I will enumerate some of them that really need to be told more fully: the growth of the church in Wigan, Bonsall taking on a full-time children's evangelist, developing Born to Grow, being asked to look after the children's work at our national conference, designing a computer game called Panic, making the first commercial video in our Fellowship, writing and editing the children's pages in our national magazine, the introduction of "Vic the Sleuth," a cartoon character, taking on and growing a business that became of national renown, the opening of soup kitchens, food banks, and night shelters, and so much more still to be relayed.

Really, I want to finish now to start Part II of this book that tells of the most fantastic adventure of my life that I was about to be thrust into—an adventure that makes me pinch myself every day as I see the goodness and miraculous hand of God working. Through it, a change has begun in our nation, which I believe will take the Church from being irrelevant to being very relevant to government, local and national. I believe it will bring about radical changes in our society and take the Church of Christ to a prominent position, as it should be, in the well-being of our nation.

Jesus said, "If I be lifted up, I will draw all men to Me." I believe that we are now at the entrance to that lifting up of Jesus in our nation.

See you soon.

Part II

Green Pastures

Chapter 1

Today is the 28th December, 2021, and I am 79 years old. I want to tell you this has been the best year of my life and you can read about it at the end of this part of my story, but now it is the time to tell you about the beginnings of Green Pastures, a ministry to house of the poor and needy that God laid on our hearts in 1999.

In the year 1992, I felt a strange impression that the Lord wanted me to move to Southport, a large seaside town in the northwest of England. I had felt this impression thirty years earlier, but now I recognised more fully when the Spirit of God was moving in my life. I decided to write to the current minister of the AOG Church in Southport, an elderly spinster named Miss Cloak, who had just turned 80 years old. I told her that I had felt God speak to me about helping her in the ministry. She sent a positive reply, and we made arrangements for me to visit her. The agreed morning arrived and duly I set off from my home in Wigan and travelled to Southport.

The church was situated on Argyle Road, which earlier in the century, had been known as Millionaire's Row. It was a large Victorian building with sweeping grounds and a high wall surrounding the curtilage. The house had two main gates with a connecting drive, two large wooden gates on each entrance, and a large garage to the side. As one approached the house, steps flanked by two large ornate pots ascended to a columned portico and a front door consisting of two large green doors leading into an inner door with a stained-glass window and stained-glass panels either side. In front of the green doors was a large mat with the name 'SANDAL' on it, the name of the house.

I rang the bell and it was opened by a very slight lady of about four feet eleven inches tall. She looked to be in her eighties. She ushered me into the vestibule, which had an immense staircase with a beautiful newel post complete with a Victorian lamp and a woven wool carpet with decorative border at all the edges. This border went around the base of the stairs and was specially created for the house by the original owners.

The lady climbed the stairs to announce my arrival, and then returned and took me up to the first floor where there was a very opulent apartment. We entered the lounge, which had a large ornate fireplace and a good deal of very smart antique furniture. I was to learn later that the furniture had been included in the sale of the property to the church. It had been created by the well-known furniture maker of the time, Lamb, chosen by the owner when the building was originally built.

Miss Cloak stood to greet me and held in her right hand a very ornate black ebony cane with a silver top. She offered me a seat and I sat down. The lady who had brought me in, whose name I discovered was Marie Shadbolt, left the room. I asked if we could pray together before we began chatting, and she agreed. After praying, she began to speak about my correspondence with her and how she had felt the communication was of the Lord. She explained that for a lady of her age, she had major surgery a month earlier to remove her gall bladder, and on the day my letter arrived, she was convalescing in her niece's caravan. She then informed me that two days earlier while she was praying, she had felt the Holy Spirit say to her, "Write to Peter Cunningham and ask him to come and help you."

Well! You can imagine my surprise when she mentioned this. Of course, the Lord is always one step ahead of us, but for her to remember me after my last visit, which has been thirty years previously, surely this could only be of the Lord. I agreed that I would come and help, commencing within the next month. We also agreed on a salary which would help to provide for my family, and I would begin to look for a property in the area.

I then began my ministry in the AOG Southport church which had called itself the Church of the Latter Rain. I was told by friends that seaside towns were the graveyard of an elderly minister (I was fifty-three at that time), and one should never go to a church where most of the congregation had one foot in the grave. I had now accomplished both. I was in a seaside town and the congregation consisted of eight spinsters, the youngest of whom was called Ellen, a

76-year-old who had been born again from prostitution. The other seven were all octogenarians.

The church in its activities was quite unique as we had a set pattern of doing things. Every night the gates were closed at 5 p.m. and the premises looked decidedly unfriendly and unwelcoming. If it had had a big notice saying 'Keep Out,' I would not have been surprised. The church sign itself was unique in that it was a picture of the cross with red blood flooding, and many of the townfolk believed the church was a cult of some sort. Everything within was pristine and ship-shape. If so much as a cup was left on the draining board, any of the members who saw it would condemn the person who had left it and declare it a mortal sin.

After being *in situ* for six weeks, I asked the dear Almighty why ever He had sent me to this church. Was I such a failure in my life? Would I end my days here paying for the sins of my past? As always, God knows the way we will take and His plans for us. He knew that His will would bring blessing to the town, the region, and eventually to the four nations of the United Kingdom. So began the new adventure in serving Christ.

The final thing that must be noted is that some thirty years earlier when I was training for the ministry, Miss Cloak had approached the minister I was training under and said that she would like me to come and take over the church. She had been informed, however, that if I did arrive, I would spoil the pristine church that she was running and would have young people sliding up and down the bannisters and causing mayhem in the church community. So Miss Cloak had decided against my coming. Now she had just invited me to come and help run the church.

Unbeknown to her, all that had been prophesied about me would come to pass, because within two years we had a youth work which had sixty young people in it and the congregation had grown to forty. The first major change that took place was the doubling of the congregation with the arrival of my family, Linda my wife and our six wonderful children, Dawn, our youngest at twelve years old, and our oldest, John, at twenty-four, with Simon, Andy, Susie, and Nathan between.

There is not sufficient time to note all the things that happened in those first few years, but some are worth noting. Danny Tuakli was really good with the young people, and he graciously agreed to become our youth leader and move with his family, wife and three girls, to Southport. I had known Danny from when he gave his life to Christ in Bonsall Camp at the age of thirteen. He had helped me pioneer the church in Bramley, Leeds, when he was eighteen, and had helped with the Bonsall Camp ministry in a wonderful way. What a wonderful work he did as the youth leader in Southport!

I can't remember how we grew, but we certainly did. We called the youth group 'The Cellar,' because that is where it was held. The house had a huge cellar area flagged with stone flags, and we filled it with settees and equipment. The kids loved it. By the end of two years, we had over sixty young people between the age of eleven and sixteen, and some of them came to Christ as Lord and Saviour.

The first young person who came to a Sunday morning service was Annabel, who lived in the Salvation Army Hostel, located fairly near to us. The difference in thinking between the new people in the church and our spinsters was huge. When Annabel arrived on the first Sunday, she was wearing tight black Lycra shorts. After the service, Miss Cloak began speaking to her and then called me over. She said, "Pastor Cunningham, I have just been telling this young lady that her shorts are of the Devil." What a great way to influence young people to love and follow Jesus!

We were joined by two wonderful women, both called Yvonne. Each was passionate about winning souls for Jesus, and so began our outreach to the homeless in the town. We opened a night shelter from the Christmas season to the end of March. We first opened it in the old Promenade Hospital and then moved to St. Luke's Hall. Yvonne Powell eventually opened the first homeless charity to house people, renting a shop with accommodation above it on East Bank Street under her own charity which the church supported.

As a church, we had a wonderful opportunity to attract people passing by. We had opened up the side wall creating a new entrance into the building, as the actual meeting hall for the church was an extension built onto the back of the Victorian building, big enough to hold fifty people. This entrance had double doors with a ramp and steps leading to it. One Sunday morning, a middle-aged man came and asked if we were the Elim Church, and I advised him that we were an AOG Church. He said, "I have heard of those. My family has just moved into the area, I think I will give you a try." Grant, his wife, and three children remained with us for the next ten years.

During 1996, Miss Cloak went to heaven, and Linda and the family moved into the flat that had now been vacated on the first floor. The other problem we were still having was a lack of musicians. Then, wonderfully, John and Hazel Rawlings and their daughter came to join us. Hazel's father had been a wonderful evangelist and had seen many, many healings in Manchester, and she had played the piano for them in their early ministry. The meeting hall had the blessing of a beautiful grand piano and Hazel took to it like a duck to water and began to use her ministry for the benefit of the church.

Chapter 2

The next few years saw growth in the youth, Sunday school, and church – but more surprisingly, our work among the homeless. My heart had always been stirred with compassion to help the homeless. But now that we were running a night shelter and involved with Yvonne on East Bank Street, more people in need came knocking on the door.

By this time, Marie had been moved to a pensioner's bungalow in Marshside. Danny and his family had their own home, and we were able to house a young woman suffering from Huntington's Chorea. This is a terminal illness which reduces your mental capacity over a number of years, and death is early in life. She came with her two-year-old daughter, Eleanor, into the ground floor flat. They had support around them, and the church congregation also supported the family. It was not unusual for Eleanor to be in the arms of one of the congregants on a Sunday evening and, when asleep, taken to her flat. The mother remained until the Social Services moved her and then, at her death, little Eleanor, a beautiful, blonde little girl, was taken to be reared by her grandmother.

We also took in a lady with mental health problems

and her two daughters. She was being evicted, and we had the opportunity to help give her a secure and safe place to live. They moved into the attic flat vacated by Marie, and the church family took care of the family alongside the local mental health team.

We would often serve as a taxi for the girls to get to school. This would generally be Vicki Woodley, a new member of the church who began helping with admin in the office and other ministries. Vicki had joined us after two divorces and, in a very delicate state, she often ran out of the services in tears. As the time passed and she felt secure with us and carried more responsibility, she became a strong member of the church, joining the leadership team, the worship team, taking care of the admin for the tenancies, and being my personal assistant.

More people began to knock at the door for help of many kinds. Often it was just to get advice and be pointed in the right direction for their needs. Others needed to be housed, and we began to have people around the building sleeping under the roof of the church.

We had one lady who would only eat organic food. She had been living in a house converted into flats without proper planning, and the landlord had moved her from the garden flat to an unsuitable flat on the upper floor that was not finished and had robbed her of many of the antique clothes that she had collected during her life. She was from Devon and was an old-fashioned ladylike woman with mental health problems.

We took her in, and she slept in the fellowship room. One of our staff helped her cook the food she loved. She was quite demanding. Over the time she was with us, she became incontinent, and we tried to get help with her but the powers that be seemed to not be able to persuade her to wash. One of our own ladies came and took on the job to clean her up. She was eventually housed in suitable accommodation at a cost of £800 a week.

We had been clients of the Community Service, a national project run by the Prison Service for people who have committed crimes but were not sent to prison. They are asked to do "community service" for a certain number of hours, 100, 150, 250, etc.

Billy was employed by the Prison Service to look after these men who would work in their local community, helping charities with different projects. Billy supervised those who arrived at our church, and they did much work around the church building to tackle necessary jobs. God had a way of bringing the skill we needed as we needed it.

Those skilled in brick work helped us take the wall 'round the building down to a lower height, making us more visible to the community. They helped add a kitchen area to the garage, which then served as a place for those on Community Service to sit and have tea and lunch, etc. They did many other jobs during Billy's time with us.

We had this service for several years, but then it was only accessible if you paid, so we stopped using them. During that time, we added a new sign to invite people to services and changed the name of the church to 'Argyle Road Church,' which we felt was more friendly to those passing by.

As time passed, the garage became home to several homeless young men who came to our door. The first was a young Englishman who had become Hindu and called himself Sheven (God of War). We connected with his grandmother, and he eventually went back to her. Before leaving, he told us he had changed his name to Vishnu (The God of Peace). We feel we had some influence on this young man.

After him came another young man with very strange habits. He wore a blanket round his shoulders and a metal hanger was hooked in his nose. He was very timid, not a threat to anyone, but odd. We did our best to care for him.

At one stage, we were given a caravan. Just as it was parked in the drive, we met two brothers who were sleeping under the pier, and so they moved into the caravan. They had come from Glasgow. One was seventeen, the other was twenty-eight. The younger began to come to our youth work and fell in love with one of the girls. Some two years later, we married them, and as the ground floor flat was again vacant, the first period of their married life was spent there. We still house him and his wife and have cared for their three children.

Each morning, I would knock on the window and rally them up with a cheerful, "It's time to pray," and they would join our prayer meeting at 9 a.m. This had been established for a few years and was attended by about eight or so of us daily.

After the brothers moved on, we housed three more

young men with various degrees of success. We had a young man join us on his return from working in Canada. It soon became obvious that he was divorced from his wife who was still living in Southport with his two children. He had been born again during his time in Canada and was now passionate to serve God. We encouraged him to visit his family and seek to re-establish his role as a father to his children. To our amazement and delight, it rekindled love in his heart for his ex-wife, who also felt love for him, and they arranged to remarry in that same year. They added two more children to their family.

There were so many other things that were happening during this period of time, and I have forgotten to mention that we bought a large second-hand window. We then took off the garage door, bricked up the opening, and put in the second-hand window. This was how the garage was when Community Services created their retreat space. When they left, it became a bedsit for the street people who continually knocked at our door.

We continued in this way for approximately three years. We were blessed in seeing lives changed and people coming to know Christ. Everyone that joined the church became active in one way or another, really being the Church in the community.

We opened up a children's work called JIM (Jesus In Me) Juniors, which grew so large that we hired the local cinema on a Saturday morning. We had 150 kids coming regularly. Thank God for the many children I had! Two of the older boys became active in leading the kids' work with their two cousins, as my brother and sister-in-law had moved to Southport to join us with his family. The work with Yvonne Powell continued to grow and the bedsits above the property in East Bank Street began to fill again with street people. Surely, the hand of God was with us.

Chapter 3

After three years, there came a knock on the front door. Two well-dressed gentlemen asked if they could have a word with us concerning the people we were housing. It turned out that they were from Sefton Borough Council and were from the planning office. Unbeknown to us, what we had been doing by housing people in the church and garage was illegal and broke the law.

They were very kind and polite and told us how the chief executive, Graham Heywood, was really impressed by what we were trying to achieve. We did know our CEO, the most senior civil servant in the borough, because he had become interested in the night shelter and had appointed the deputy director of housing to help us in not only securing our base in the old Promenade Hospital but also providing for us certain funds and bedding. So, it came as no surprise that his consideration of the work we were doing at Sandal was commendable in the fact that we were caring for people, but the way we were achieving it was not permissible.

They went on to explain that what we were doing was illegal and that we would have to remove anyone on the premises who was not a legal tenant. Our tenanted flats were perfectly legal and would remain in our care. So, with a heavy heart, one by one, our friends were removed from the property, and the caravan moved from the car park.

The two gentlemen from the council also informed us that the local authority was seeking a £900,000 grant from the European Common Market Fund to improve the sea front in Dukes Ward and that the officers of the Common Market had insisted that 10 percent of the grant would go towards housing homeless and marginalised people as the Ward was considered a deprived area. They then went on to ask if we would help provide information for the document the council was preparing to submit to enable the bid to go forward, which we were only too willing to do. Anything to ensure that those we knew Jesus wanted us to care for could be helped. Our hearts of compassion and love for these homeless and marginalised people often brought us to weeping for them and a desire to house and bring comfort to them.

I am writing this narrative on the third of January, 2022. Some five nights ago on the twenty-eight of December, 2021, I was deprived of sleep during the night and began to pray and seek God. My heart was strangely moved with compassion over many things, but the Lord brought to remembrance several wonderful things that had happened in the past. So, at this moment, I would like to tell you some of the changes that we were seeing take place at that time in our ministry.

From the time the council officers asked us to help until three years later were some of the most exciting, adventurous, and faith-filled moments of our lives. My son Andrew, my friend Vicki Woodley, and myself embarked on setting up what would become Green Pastures, and these are just two of the stories that took place in those early years.

We housed a man who was a rampant alcoholic who never washed, whose smell was almost intolerable, and whose life was full of anger and his mouth full of expletives like a sewer. We housed him in February and almost every other day, he visited our office in Sandal. He'd call me "F**ing B" as he greeted me and expressed his anger to us on a regular basis. All we could do was love this man, care for him, and show him the compassion of Christ. Month in, month out, we loved and cared for this difficult person.

One day in June, a beautiful sunny morning, I left Sandal and saw the man, Billy, sitting on the steps. I sat down one step higher than him. My knees were at his eye level. The sun was warm, the day beautiful, I was at peace within my heart. How the conversation began I cannot now recollect, but I do know what Billy said to me. "I just want to tell you why I am such a terrible person. Nine years ago, I returned home from work to learn the terrible news that my daughter had been killed in a road accident. She was my only child, and you can imagine that my wife and I loved her dearly. She was 11 years old and just changing from being a child into being a young woman. She was clever, bright, so full of laughter."

Then he reached inside his jacket and pulled out this picture, 6" x 4", of what I can only say was a picture of a beautiful young girl who I could see was beginning to change into the maturity of womanhood. Her hair was as black as a raven's wing and her deep brown eyes were like pools of laughter and her smile was one to die for. She truly was one of the most beautiful young girls I have seen. He said, "This is a picture of my daughter that died nine years ago." Then he turned and looked into my face, and said, "I want to tell you, you are the first group of people that have showed me kindness over such a long period of time, and this is the first time I have been able to open up and talk of those tragic events that took place nine years ago. I want to thank you for caring for me." I asked if I could pray with him, and he said he would love me to pray for him.

From that moment, this man began to recover and change. After six months he was a totally changed person and in twelve months he had fallen in love with a lovely lady, and they married and moved from Southport. What has happened to them since, I don't know, but I do know that when a Christian shows the loving kindness of Christ and the compassion of the Lord to those in desperate need, miracles do take place. We now have hundreds of stories like this after serving the Lord for the last twenty-one years.

There is one more story I would like to relate. We came across a couple in their late thirties who were living in total squalor in a container wagon behind Tesco in Kew. We had recently purchased Derby Road, which I will come back to later. We housed them at 6 Derby Road in a flat, and I began to have conversations with Pam about the Lord Jesus, that no matter where we came from or what we had done, He loved her, and if she would confess her sin, He would forgive her and she would begin life anew.

Pam and her partner were both heroin addicts. Pam was not an unattractive woman, and the way she paid for her "fix" was by prostitution. Not that she wanted to be a prostitute, but it was the only way of maintaining her habit and that of her partner.

After some nine months, I really began to feel that there was a possibility of Pam coming to Christ. She had softened in her attitude towards Christ and was asking searching questions about whether the Lord could really forgive a woman who was living such a sinful life. She was so close to the Kingdom, so very close.

In Southport, over the years, the sand had blown off the beach and grass had grown and created quite high sand dunes. The local authority had created walkways on these dunes by putting slats of wood about a meter wide that were joined together by rope as pathways so that people could walk the dunes. One Monday morning, someone came into the office and broke the awful news that Pam had been murdered and her body had been stuffed ignominiously under one of the walkways on the sand dunes.

At moments like this, it breaks your heart to hear that someone close to you has been murdered. You don't quite know what to do, so you leave the room where you are, find a quiet place, and begin to weep and ask the dear Almighty why this had taken place to someone so near to His Kingdom.

At that time, some of the churches had begun to pray together at 7:30 each Tuesday, so the next day I found myself in the prayer meeting with many other Christians from other churches. One of the members from Christ Church approached me and said, "I thought you would like to know that Pam, who you housed in Derby Road, was in our church on Sunday morning, and when the appeal was made, she went forward to give her life to Christ." I wept for joy remembering the thief on the cross to whom Jesus said, "This day, you will be with me in paradise. I had the joy of knowing that when I go to heaven, I will see Pam there, a brand plucked as it were from the burning, now in the presence of Christ for the rest of eternity.

These are just two of the incidents that took place in the time I am writing of. Let me say, in conclusion, the bid for £900,000 was accepted by the Common Market and duly arrived with the local authority in Sefton. I then had a meeting with Graham Heywood, the Chief Executive, and asked if he would like us, as the charity who had helped him procure £900,000, to help him spend the money wisely. He said to me, "We are the professionals. We know how to spend the money wisely." With my tongue in my cheek, I wanted to say, "Yes, local authorities do know how to spend money." In this case, I did not think it was spent wisely.

They opened a one-stop shop for those seeking accommodation as the council did not have such a facility in the town. They used £250,000. The rest they spent with a preferred partner, a housing association. As a partnership, they renovated flats above the shops in Lord Street to rent to people who needed accommodation, but not to one person from under the pier, or golf course, or park. The ones that we had dedicated ourselves to help, those that were the most marginalised in our community, not one of them was housed. To say the least, I was quite cross. The Scripture says, "I know the plans I have for you" (Jeremiah 29:11a), and little did I realise that the dear Almighty had plans for us, which were much greater that we could have ever hoped or thought of and were more amazing than our wildest dreams.

PETE CUNNINGHAM

Chapter 4

We rose to pray the next morning, as we were doing this daily now and reading the Scriptures systematically. I need to tell you that, at times, I am not the best Christian on the planet, and this was one of the times when my Christian spirit was not at its peak. I came in moaning to the dear Almighty about the fact that not a penny of the £900,000 allocated for looking after the poor and the marginalised was going to be spent on those that were under the pier. I continued by saying, "God, what are you doing? Why isn't this happening? We spent a lot of valuable time producing the paperwork to achieve this £900.000." Then, as we sat together, we began to read the Scripture reading for the day, Luke 10, and in this chapter, you find the parable of the Good Samaritan. Let me remind you that this is Christ teaching us about who our neighbour is and how we should love that neighbour without reserve. As we began to read, the Holy Spirit began to open the Scripture to us.

Let me say that I am very dim sometimes at understanding God's Word. I may read a passage fifty or one hundred times and suddenly it lights up to me. It was so on this morning. As we read the story, a man who was not a Christian finds this other man, beaten and left for dead by the road-side. Two others had already passed by, both of them had been men of faith; but here this man who was not of the faith, stopped, got off his donkey, got out his "first aid kit," ministered to the unconscious person by the road, put him on his own donkey, took him to the local inn where he booked him a bed, and then it appears, sat up all night nursing him. Then as he left in the morning, he gave the innkeeper enough to care for the man for the next two weeks, taking the money out of his own purse. He then said to the man, "If I owe you any further, I will pay you when I come again."

Suddenly, the Holy Spirit lit up this last part of Christ's story, revealing this man's heart of compassion and love for his fellow traveller. This Samaritan, committed himself to caring for the wellbeing of this man until he was fully recovered, and he was willing to put his hand in his own pocket and pay. We don't know if the man had a relapse and was there for six weeks or if after two weeks he was fully recovered; all we do know is that this Samaritan took total responsibility for a stranger he had never met.

What a challenge to us on that morning! We felt the Lord say to us, "I never asked you to go to the local authority with a begging bowl. I gave you the responsibility of taking care of the poor and marginalised in your local society. You have abrogated your responsibility that I have given to my Church to care for the homeless and marginalised and have handed it over to local and national government, who have made a complete pig's ear of it, and you have failed in the task

I have given to you. Am I not the God of all the Earth? Do I not own all the cattle on a thousand hills? Can I not provide for your need? Am I impoverished and bankrupt? Surely I am the God who will provide all your needs according to my riches in glory."

Talk about feeling admonished by the Almighty. It certainly was a wakeup call to a small church to respond to the call of God to what He had told us to do. So we said to the Lord, "What shall we do?" This seemed to be quite a logical question, "What shall we do, Lord?" And we felt the Lord reply to us, "What did he do?" He put his hand in his own pocket. "Put your hand in your own pocket and help my needy ones in your community."

Now at that moment in time I had a small pension of £6000 to help in my retirement. Vicki Woodley had some property that was part of her divorce settlement which gave her a rental income. She said to us, "I will raise a loan on my property and put that in a sum of £25k." My son who was on a limited income said, "Whatever I have left of my wages at the end of the month I will put that in." Between us we gathered £31k and £100 gift every month from Andy. This, at that moment of time, would buy very little in Southport; however, God had plans.

A member of our church came to us having known that our desire was to buy a property to house these drug addicts and alcoholics we found under the pier and elsewhere. He said, "I have a friend who is selling a property built in the late twenties comprised of two flats, but it suffers from subsidence and is not mortgageable. He will accept £25k for it." So, Vicki, Andy and I went to view it. Let me say, we were all a little disappointed as the subsidence was so great, this detached property looked like the Titanic on land. It was sloping at such an angle that one would assume over the next three months, it would disappear altogether into the ground.

Andy at that time was working in an architect's office and by good fortune was able to ask a structural engineer to take a look. The good news was that all the movement had occurred prior to 1940 and so it was liable to remain in its present state for the next one hundred years. We agreed to purchase the property.

I must admit at that moment in time I was Doubting Thomas himself; I complained to the Almighty, stating the fact that as we would put alcoholics into these flats, they would destroy the property. It would not go up in value but would more than likely go down in value as these people would most probably kick the front door in if they lost their key. If they got angry, they may punch holes in the internal walls and, not being used to having a kitchen, it would be damaged in the first three months. Clothes would not be washed and the washing up would pile up to the ceiling.

Then the Lord reminded me of the story of the wedding of Cana and how Mary had said to the servants in John 2, "Whatsoever He tells you to do, do it." He reminded me that the head steward plunged his jug into a water pot full of water and drew it out. Then he walked down the aisle where the guests were seated, his heart pounding as he carried that jug of water, and climbed onto the raised platform where the bride and groom, their close relatives, and the head of the feast sat. Most probably he was saying in his mind, "I am going to get the sack because I have a jug of water to pour out into this man's wine glass." Only when he began to pour that water did it turn into the most exquisite wine that the host of the feast had ever tasted. I felt at that moment the Lord say, "Just trust me." This was the beginning of our venture of faith.

The first tenant we decided to put in was, I would say, a rampant alcoholic who was living under the pier. He had a sad story of the breakup of his family and a very fractious divorce, which left him with his wife denying him access to their children. This had caused him to hit the bottle so badly that he lost his job and ended up under the pier. Now, at that time, we knew a couple of solicitors personally in the town, and our thinking was that for his wife to exclude him from seeing his children was, in fact, breaking the law, unless this man was mistreating his children. If one of our solicitors would take up the man's case on a pro bono basis, we may win him access to his children, which could improve his mental state of health. With this thought in mind, we placed him in the top flat.

Now before we could consider the next person to put into the ground floor flat, a two-bedroom flat, we were approached by another church in Southport. Let me say, we had begun to have quite good relationships with the other evangelical churches in the town and had set up a monthly meeting, which we called, the Ministers Fraternal. It was one of the member churches that approached us with a request for housing. They had a young woman in her early twenties who was a single parent, who had a three-month-old baby. She was renting a caravan from them to live in. Unfortunately, one half of the roof of the caravan had sunken down and was letting water in. They were both therefore living in the dry half of the caravan. They had approached the local authority to see if they could be re-housed, but were informed that although they were in need, it wasn't urgent since they could still live in the place they were renting. "Could the church please have the ground floor flat to accommodate this needy family."

You can imagine that our hearts were stirred by the story, and our belief was that we are one Body. The flat was duly rented to this member of their church who had not come to know Christ at that moment. They were trusting in hope that she would make that decision for Christ.

For the next nine months, we looked after our alcoholic upstairs and our friends looked after the young lady downstairs. To our delight, a solicitor accepted the brief and within three months our tenant had access to his children. Vicki, who had in a previous life looked after a good number of rental properties, took charge of making sure that the right forms were filled in so that the local authority would pay due rent which came directly to us.

Vicki said one morning, "Can we call this operation Green Pastures?" I was a little taken aback. I thought, "Why call it Green Pastures?" So, I asked the question, "Why Green Pastures?" She replied, "I have always wanted to bring peace and tranquillity to those who are marginalised." What could we say other than "yes"? This was indeed our ambition, to bring change to those who we hoped to help into the future.

Now our gentleman living in the top flat, being able to have his children come to stay brought an amazing change into his life. By the end of six months, he had not only got off the booze but had got back into work. We were absolutely delighted. The Lord had really helped us. Our only concern was the council had now stopped paying rent to us as the tenant was working and we wondered if he would be honourable and continue to pay the rent out of his wages. To our delight the rent kept coming in. We were over the moon. Although he had not become a Christian, his life had become so much better.

Then after nine months, to our surprise, both tenants phoned us up and told us they wished to terminate their tenancies. As we were doing so well with them, we wondered if we had offended them in some way and we arranged for them to come in and see us to discuss the end of their tenancies.

When they arrived, they were holding hands. They said, "We have fallen in love and we are getting married and we are going to rent a three bedroomed house for us to live in."

What a great joy and delight for us to see these lives made whole and restored! The only thing that remained was for us to fall on our knees to thank God for what had happened and sincerely apologise for our doubt that He could change the worst people into the best. He does far more abundantly than we can ask or think.

Chapter 5

After the success that the Lord had brought to pass with the first two tenants that we had housed, we felt so encouraged that, before the end of the year, we bought two more properties and were housing nine people.

We had paid £25k for the first property, and the next one was a semi-detached house which was just about 400 meters from our first property. It was owned by a widower in his sixties. His wife had died some twelve years earlier and, in some ways, this loss had destroyed his zest for life.

When we viewed the property, which was on the market for £27k, it was in an extremely poor state of repair. It looked like it hadn't been cleaned for the last twelve years and the garden, which would be approximately forty meters long, was so overgrown we wondered if there were lions and tigers in the dense undergrowth. The pine trees that had been planted no more than four meters from the back of the house were so huge that they virtually blocked light from the kitchen, but again the cost was so low that we could not resist buying this.

Within six weeks, with help from friends, the trees were cut down, the garden cleared, the house cleaned and decorated, and a needy family was placed in it. This dear lady and her son began to come to church. This turned out to be a great success as, within four years, this lady would go back to full time education at Edge Hill College, train as a teacher, pass her exams, and begin teaching in one of the local schools. She eventually moved back to Halifax, her hometown, to teach there.

One morning Vicki came into the office extremely excited. She said, "I have found our third property and I really believe the Lord wants us to buy it." A thrill of excitement went through me as I knew this godly woman was truly believing that God had spoken to her about the third property we were to purchase. So, without delay, I suggested that we at least go immediately to see the outside of the property. We climbed into Vicki's car and set off.

As we proceeded on our way, I noticed that we were entering into one of the more expensive areas of the town. Then we turned in the road where the house was located, which has extremely large detached three story properties. She brought the car to a stop outside one of these houses. Outside was a hand painted 'For Sale' sign. When I say hand-painted, it was very crudely put together, a rectangular piece of plywood which had hand-painted upon it the words, 'For Sale.' The paint had been put on so thickly that there were runs of paint through the letters.

Vicki had spoken to the owner of the property and discovered that the house as it stood was home to the owner's mum who lived in the garden flat and was now ill and needed to be cared for. Her daughter lived in the attic flat and was about to relocate. She had lived on the first floor which was arranged as bedsits, and she cared for 3 adults with low key mental health issues but had closed this work down due to her mother's illness. She was very happy to think we also would be helping people in our venture with the house.

I looked at Vicki and asked the question, "Is this the house?" She replied, "Yes."

My next question was obvious, "How much is it?" Vicki, without batting an eyelid, replied, "£166k."

One hundred and sixty-six thousand pounds! After I caught my breath, I said, "Remember we had paid £25k for the first property and £27k for our second. This was a huge jump in our expectations."

I had forgotten that God had said to us, "Am I not the God of all the earth? Do I not own all the cattle on a thousand hills?"

Now you must remember, that at this point in time, the three of us were really just novices in helping the homeless. We didn't even realise that the properties had to be registered in someone's name. At our first purchase, the solicitor politely asked, "Whose name is this property going into?" Also, we had not thought of mortgages until we purchased the second property. A friend advised us that we could possibly get a Buy to Let mortgage and introduced us to a financial advisor, named Tim, who still helps us to this day. So, we had taken a mortgage on our second property on which we had been able to get together the deposit required through our credit cards. We were now aware that we were able to have Buy to Let mortgages on any future property we needed to buy. However, £156k was a big leap from our first two purchases. A leap of faith was needed, and we decided to leap and buy the big house.

Because we had upgraded our second purchase so dramatically, we were able to go back to the mortgage company and remortgage the house and use the new funds as a deposit on the big house. So, we cobbled together enough money to purchase the property. What an exciting day that was when we got the keys, as the possibility in this property was six self-contained flats!

There was a deal of work to do before we could achieve our aim. Vicki and I, with the help of a few of the members of our church, and the unexpected arrival of a self-employed Christian builder from Buxton, began to make the changes.

The garden flat was already self-contained. On the ground floor, alterations were needed and the same on the second floor. The third floor had a two-bed, self-contained flat. We ended up with a garden flat in the basement with level access to the back garden. On the ground floor, a one-bedroom flat with a massive lounge stretching from the front to the back of the building, and a studio flat. On the first floor, a two-bedroomed flat, another studio flat, and a self-contained flat in the attic area.

Within days of completion, the house had become almost a women's refuge. What a fantastic opportunity we had of ministering Christ to the people we were housing.

As over the years we have housed thousands of tenants just in Southport, a story on everyone would be a step too far, but the odd story will illustrate the variety of persons and situations we have come across. I will just expand on one of the first tenants in this house.

We were called by one of the church members to ask if we could help a lady and her daughter who were living in a very damp and unsuitable flat. We agreed to take her on and began the necessary procedures, the first of which was to visit her and see what we needed to move to our property.

We entered the flat and found that it was full of "stuff" on every surface. She was a hoarder. We found "stuff" in the lounge on top of the ironing board and in the bath and bathroom. We began the task of moving her belongings. As she wouldn't part with anything, we used the church minibus. We filled it many times but decided with her agreement that we would put all her non-required items in the large front bedroom in as neat and tidy a way as we could.

We made many trips up and down and when we thought we had completed the task, with all her essentials in the kitchen lounge and bedroom, which she would share with her young child, she said that we had not taken everything. On returning to the flat, in one of the rooms where there was a low sloping roof, there was a wall about twelve feet and there was a curtain across. Behind this curtain were more black bags full of stuff.

We moved the remaining items and at last she was relocated and has lived there ever since. The room is still her storage place, and her daughter has moved away. The rest of her flat is pretty full, but she is as happy as she can be and has been safe for almost twenty years. These three purchases were in our first year of existence as housing the homeless.

Now let us begin our second year. The number of people still living under the pier and elsewhere amounted to some twenty rough sleepers. Their need was a great burden on hearts that we felt we must eradicate. We then encountered a local landlord who wanted to sell three of his rented properties, which contained eighteen flats, only seven of which were occupied. This meant there were eleven free spaces to fill, and at that moment in time, we couldn't raise the £250k required to purchase.

The landlord was keen to sell and we were keen to buy, so we agreed to give him a £20k deposit to lease the building for a year and finalise the purchase at the end of the year. How overjoyed we were to be able to make a large hole in the number of people sleeping rough by acquiring this property. We shook hands on the deal in the afternoon and I went home feeling like I had entered heaven. We hadn't got the money; we were trusting God that He would supply all our needs. So, I went to bed that night excited by the new adventure we had just begun.

All eleven flats would need renovation, including painting and decorating. After the work we had already accomplished at the big house, we were certain that within a six-month period we would have these properties ship-shape and in Bristol fashion.

I couldn't sleep and so by 7:30 a.m. I was off to survey the promised land, our new venture at the site. To my amazement, when I arrived the whole of Flat Number 6 had been cordoned off by blue and white police tape. I stopped the car and went across the road to where a policeman was standing. I asked him why the building had been taped off. He explained that in the bottom flat, two men had been murdered; in fact, they had been beaten to death by a golf club. It had been a place where drugs were regularly dealt and an argument had arisen which had caused this terrible act of violence.

I don't know how you would feel in discovering that the property you had just agreed to lease and then purchase had been a place for drug deals, but I went from the height of ecstasy to the depths of despair in a moment of time. I could not believe that the Almighty had allowed this to happen. In fact, I was shocked that God had allowed us to enter into this agreement knowing that this was about to take place.

I got into my car, drove home, entered my bedroom, fell on my knees, and said to the Almighty, "God, what are you doing? No one will want to live here now. We have committed ourselves to spend another £230k which we don't have. We will have to see our houses to pay the debt. We will have to go bankrupt." I was in the depths of despair.

Now it is not often I feel that God speaks to me, but after I had bewailed my disappointment to the Almighty, I felt the Lord answer me. "Do you not think I do not know what I am doing? This is not your business, it is mine. I am going to turn back the corner of the tapestry I am weaving so you might understand my purposes in your life. You have just invaded the darkest place in your town, and My intention is to turn that house into a place of light and peace and bring that to the people that you house." I felt relief sweep over me and that my faith in God would rise to see this accomplished.

If you go to the site now and meet the people there, although they are mainly alcoholics we house, it is like a family, the people living there do not want to move on as they relate well to one another. Andrew, my son, visited there a couple of years ago with one of our pastoral care workers. He met a man still in bed at mid-day. Danny, our pastoral care worker had saved this man's life after he had had an epileptic fit while in the bath. Andy asked him how he liked living in the property. He said, "Paradise."

When you trust in God, He surely does know what he is doing. The property is a wonderful place, and it truly can be paradise. It is now twenty plus years down the line, and many have experienced the love that only Christ can bring from a Christian community that truly cares for those in need.

In year three, a friend brought to our notice a property, which consisted of a one-bedroom flat and four bedsits. In January, we put an offer in of £60k. This was because any-thing over that meant we would have to pay stamp duty and would cost us a good deal more. Our offer was rejected as the owner said he had an offer of £75k. In late February, out of the blue, the owner phoned the office and said that the buyer had let him down and that, if we could purchase it before the first of April, we could have it for the £60k. Of course we were overjoyed, and as we had already negotiated with the bank and had a loan offer on the table, we knew we would be able to complete the purchase by March 31. We agreed and set in motion the mortgage with the bank.

Borrowing money by raising mortgages had now become quite commonplace to us and we were growing comfortable with dealing with our solicitors, signing documents, and moving forward knowing that we were fulfilling the purposes of God in building the Kingdom and helping those who were homeless and marginalised in our town of Southport.

Then tragedy struck! I say tragedy, perhaps tragedy and confusion, as ten days before we were due to complete on the property, the bank phoned us and said, "We didn't realise this property has four bedsits in it. We do not loan money on HMO's (Houses in Multiple Occupation)." This was a new term, HMO, and when we looked it up, we saw that it referred to any house where there were more than three bedsits. So, what could we do? Well, the answer is, you pray. We prayed and said, "God, we have committed to buying this property. We only have the £10,000 deposit; we are short £50,000. We need Your help. Please help us in our dilemma."

Two days after this prayer and ten days before we were due to complete it, we received a call from a gentleman whose wife had been to see what we were doing in January. Evidently from his conversation, she had been extremely impressed, not only with the houses that we were purchasing for the homeless, but also with the care that we were showing in the love of Christ that we were surrounding them with. He then said, "We are so delighted by what you are achieving in Southport, we have decided to loan you some money. I am running quite a successful business and in April our accounts will be sent to our accountant. When we know how much we have earned during the course of this year, we will send you a loan to help you with the work that you are doing." Then he added, "By the way, I have some money slushing away in my business account." These are the exact words he said, "Do you have any needs at this moment in time?" Well, what was slushing around in his business account was a mystery to me, but what I did know was we desperately needed £50,000. So, I said to him, "We are in desperate need of £50,000 by March 31 to complete the purchase of a house, as the bank who said they would lend us the money has let us down." His immediate reply was, "Let me have your bank details and I will Bacs it to you." So on the following Tuesday, we received the £50,000 and, on the Thursday, completed the purchase of our new property.

Now if that was not God answering our desperate plea for help, I don't know what else it could have been. His ear is ever open to our cry.

Chapter 6

Some seven years down the line, we had virtually cured street homelessness in our town for which we wish to praise God for His goodness to us in the land of the living. We were now housing approximately seventy people. A number of them had improved in their lives and had moved on, and a few of them had come to know Christ as their Lord and Saviour. We had become quite comfortable in what we were achieving. We were now employing a gentleman who helped us with our administration. Vicki now had a special day every week at the Housing Benefit Office with a member of staff who was appointed to look after all our needs and concerns with the housing benefit of our tenants.

The great thing for us was that the government has regularised housing benefits, and we knew exactly what we would receive for a bedsit, a one bed, a two bed, or a three-bed property. This made budgeting a lot easier, although every year we did make a small loss, and it was only the fact that our property grew in value year on year that kept us solvent. We were not asking anyone to give us money or looking for grants. The good thing was that Vicki had her own income, I was still being paid by the church, and Andrew was earning a wage in the architects practice where he was employed. We were in it just to serve God and to fulfil the Word of God which is that Jesus has asked us to look after the poor and needy in our community.

Partnering with another group had never entered our heads, but one day there was a knock on the door and a man called Steve introduced himself as working for a charity called North Staffs Chaplaincy. He said he and his associate Roger Howarth served as chaplains in Shrewsbury Prison had opened an independent charity called North Staffs Chaplaincy to help prisoners, who had made decisions for Christ, with independent living as they left the prison.

He then informed us that one of the offenders was about to leave prison and, when asked where he was going, he said he would like to go to Southport where a church had property and had housed him previously, and he felt that they would be willing to look after him. The reason for Steve's visit was to ask us if we would comply with that request, which of course we were glad to do. So, we arranged a date when he would arrive and, some weeks later, Steve, the young man, and Roger arrived at our door.

We were able to settle the young man in, apply for his unemployment benefit, and help with his housing benefit, and one of us took him down to settle into his accommodation. The young man was a pleasant lad, and we prayed to God to help him not to get into difficulty again.

Vicki and I sat down with Roger and Steve to talk about the work they were doing. Roger poured out his heart to us about how he loved Christ and how this had drawn him into a ministry in the prisons. A number of prisoners would come to chapel on the Sunday and then would visit their study groups during the week. Oh, the joy that he and Steve found when one of them would come to Christ and make a commitment to serve the Lord Jesus! What a blessing this was for them, but they found that after several years of working in the prison, some of those who had made commitments to Christ reoffended and returned to prison after eighteen months or two years of absence from the prison. In fact, at that moment in time, the reoffending rate in the nation was seventy percent of those people leaving prison returned in under two years.

They had opened the charity North Staff Chaplaincy so that they could arrange to meet people coming out of prison and then to help guide them in their lives. They said there were numerous people that they arranged to meet, perhaps at McDonalds, or Pizza Hut, or one of the other well known fast food restaurants in the area of Stoke-on-Trent, so that they could begin helping them with their readjustment to normal life. They told us how frustrating it was that the majority never turned up because they were homeless, and so they returned to their old habits, and the next time they saw them was when they had returned to prison after reoffending.

We were touched by this story and saddened in our hearts. These two men were no different to us in their love for the marginalised that they came across in the community, and we were near to tears as this drama unfolded.

We were drawn into the reality of prison life and these men who appeared to have no chance in life of moving forward because no opportunity was given to them in their housing requirements.

Then out of the blue after Roger had finished his dialogue of their problems, he said to us, "You don't think there is any possibility that you may be able to buy us a couple of houses?" Let me say that I was shocked by the impudence of this man I had only just met and didn't know from Adam. He had not asked us to donate £10 to his charity but was wanting to put his hand into our back pocket for one hundred and twenty thousand pounds, which would be the cost of two houses in Stoke-on-Trent at that moment in time, 2006. Again, to my surprise, my fellow labourer in the harvest field expressed her delight that they had counted us worthy of helping them in such a wonderful endeavour to change the lives of these very needy men.

Immediately as you do in these circumstances, my mouth did not open but my mind went into prayer. "God, what do we do? How do we engage with these two brothers that are certainly like us and part of our body?" Immediately, a scripture came to me, and we always base our life on what the Scriptures guide us in. The scripture was 1 John 3:17, "If your brother asks you for something and you can help him, do not shut up the bowels of your compassion."

There are some days when the word of God burns you and although you find it difficult to act upon it, because of your love Christ, you find it incumbent on your spirit to implement the work of God. Then the Lord reminded me of how our property had risen in value and at that moment in time, the mortgage companies were pressing us to borrow more money, which we did not require for Southport at that time. He then reminded me that this business was not ours but His, and He was the managing director, and the money that we had available was there to help our brothers and sisters who would come to us and ask us if we could buy property for them. So, in the moments between his asking and my replying, God had dealt with the matter in my heart and we agreed to buy him two houses which would be two bedsit houses in Stoke. For we are truly one Body, and Jesus continually reminds us that we need to work together to build His Kingdom and not to be isolated from one another. We are brothers and sisters in Christ.

We set about remortgaging two of our properties to be ready to provide deposits to purchase two properties. We then instructed Roger and Steve to go and look for property that they would like to use for their mission. Then, one Saturday in December, we drove down to view five properties. We made offers on three and, before returning home, we had agreed to buy two. Roger asked us when they will be available, to which we answered, "Within a couple of months." Roger seemed rather surprised at that. I thought that it would take longer than that.

When we deal with the local council, we expect to wait at least a year before anything is accomplished. However, we delivered the first in February and began a new chapter in the ministry of North Staff Chaplaincy. The second house was delivered in March.

To our joy and excitement, within four years this group had grown to housing 120 ex-offenders. Over half of them had come to know Christ and were attending local churches. How exciting is that! How wonderful is that! How absolutely marvellous is that! The Scripture says he that wins souls is wise. Because of the goodness of God prompting us in our service of Him, we now had become wise servants by investing in the ministry of others and releasing them in another area of the country to do the ministry to which God had called them. Now they were reaping a great harvest and we were privileged to be part of that reaping. This was the beginning of what God had planned for us to do, and over the next months and years, the Lord would do amazing things through this budding ministry.

The next unusual event in the development of our ministry was a phone call from The Times newspaper. At that time, we were just beginning to work with Housing Justice on their launch of Homeless Sunday. The phone call was to see if one of their reporters could visit us and put an article in the newspaper about homeless people. We agreed for them to visit us in Southport. They would arrive on a train at 10 a.m. in the morning at Southport Railway Station, and I would collect them.

Being a little naive when it comes to national newspapers in what they want and how they do things, I imagined that this reporter from one of the prominent national newspapers would be coming to gather information on a number of projects in the Merseyside area. Having experience with the local newspaper, who would arrive for ten or fifteen minutes and then do the report either good bad or indifferent for local consumption, I figured if we gave The Times reporter an hour and a half that should be plenty of time. So, to put the picture in full focus, we would look after the reporter from 10 a.m. to 11:30 a.m. after which my day would be free.

We had just housed the last street person in Southport some days previously, and as my custom was to visit our new tenants within the first fortnight of them moving into their accommodation, I arranged to reach our tenant, who had a major problem of alcoholism, at midday.

The morning arrived and I met a charming lady in her early forties who was the reporter from The Times. She was dressed in what appeared to be an expensive suit and, as you would expect from a lady of culture, she smelt as though she had bathed in Chanel No. 5. She was extremely articulate and, feeling rather nervous, I greeted her and welcomed her to Southport, put her in the car, climbed in next to her, and commenced the journey back to the office.

I asked her politely what time her train was back to Wigan to catch the London train. She said she would be leaving at 7 p.m. I was a little startled at this as this was far from my planning for the day. Again, I politely said, "What are you going to be doing for the day?"

She replied instantly, "I will be with you for the day."

I inwardly began to panic.

I then said, "Well, I am busy today."

She replied, "Don't worry. I will just follow you 'round."

I then had visions of a nightmare scenario as, at 12 p.m., I would be visiting our latest tenant.

One of the joys we had in Green Pastures was returning to homeless people a degree of self-esteem when we handed them their own key to the flat they would be renting. We put no restriction on them so when an alcoholic moved in, it wasn't unusual for them to be as high as a kite by 6 p.m. in the evening. Also, their ability to housekeep was virtually nil so, in my imagination, as we would enter this flat, the "tinnies" (beer cans) would be on the floor, possibly knee deep. The bed would be unmade, the bedroom would be dishevelled with dirty underwear on the floor, and the washing up piled in the sink.

In my mind, I thought this lady would come into the flat, not realising that this is how people live who have come off the street and that it was not my fault if the flat was in a bit of a bad condition. In my imagination, I thought this lady would think we are terrible landlords and go away and write an article about the appalling landlord she had met.

I then silently prayed, "God, why have You dropped me in it? How am I going to escape this problem?" She met the staff, thought they were all wonderful, and then we went off to my new friend. I am so glad that God knows the future and quite often it turns out differently from our expectations.

At midday, we knocked on the flat door of our new tenant. The door opened and of course at midday this good gentleman was just a little merry, the bed was unmade, there were "tinnies" on the floor, there was washing up in the sink and clothes on the floor. But what I had forgotten was two things. First, this lady was a reporter and was looking for a story, and the second thing was that this man was an academic. He had had a bad relationship with his lady friend which had made him turn to drink and he had ended up on the streets. In fact, he had a PhD in languages and was a college lecturer before his fall from grace.

She began to speak to him and immediately recognised that she was speaking to a cultured man, and then sat on the bed with him next to her and they talked for over an hour about where he had come from and where he was now and how he appreciated the help Green Pastures was giving him. From my heart rose tons of praise. "Thank you, God, for this wonderful, intellectual tenant that has rescued your servant from disaster."

The rest of the day, I floated along and eventually, after an evening meal, deposited this lady back on the station at Southport. She then put her arms around me and said to me, "I have never come across such a loving group of people in all my journalistic career." She then wrote a three-page article in The Times insert called "T2" and called us "God's Estate Agent." If you remember, I said she hugged me and she also smelt of Chanel No. 5. The only problem I had that evening was explaining to my wife why I smelt so good.

After the appearance of that article, we had people from Lands End to John O'Groats phoning us or emailing us and

Christian groups asking how they could help the homeless and marginalised in their town. So began the exciting journey of becoming a national social enterprise with charitable status, seeing many people come to Christ, many lives changed, and the end is not yet.

Praise God!

Epilogue

It has been nearly two decades since that article was written and many other wonderful things have taken place during that time. Other Churches and charities have joined us in this wonderful pilgrimage to bring changes to the poor and marginalised of our society.

I spoke of the best year of my life, pointing to 2021. To encourage you, despite all the difficulties of COVID, Green Pastures continued to grow. I have always believed when it is Dark in Egypt, it is Light in Goshen, the place where God's children are. In that year our lending, which we expected to fall, rose to the highest input ever. We opened our Development Department with an amazing team who worked on a new project to create from a very basic building a 21st Century Centre for the Dundonald Church in Wimbledon in which to serve their community, incorporating 18 Flats available to the local population. The team also began a programme of building homes to house the homeless. The Lord enabled us to purchase Mattersey College which was at a cost of £3 million, which God miraculously provided as we took a massive leap of faith. This has enabled us to educate those whose lives are changing so wonderfully as they come to Christ. The takeover of a dark and dreary Rehab in Derby with 27 bed spaces, brought light, change, and positivity from the locals and the local council, and again lives were changing and coming to Christ. We had 240 new bed spaces, our highest figure ever, and better relationships with CEOs of similar charities. Our GP Direct Project in Merseyside grew faster than we had ever anticipated, growing to 40 bed spaces within 18 months, and we began planning for GP Direct Manchester.

As we progress through the coming years, our dream is to end homelessness in our nation in all its many and various guises, and this continuous story will unfold as we journey together. If you are a Church Leader or a Believer and this story has touched you and you feel the Lord leading you to say, "Yes, I want to be involved in this ministry, I want to see lives changed, I want to be involved in helping the marginalised of our nation," then we are so willing to help you establish this in your town or city. We do not say the journey will be easy, but we will be there to help you every step of the way, encouraging and guiding you in your early steps towards ending homelessness in your town or city. Please contact us on our web site www.greenpastures.co.uk.

All my love in Christ,

Pastor Pete

About the Author

Pastor Pete became a Christian at the age of twenty-one after riotous teen years. He worked in stock broking from the age of sixteen to twenty-three when he entered training in the ministry. He pastored several churches, pioneering two, and he built a children's holiday camp. Having had a compassion for the marginalised all through his ministry, the Assemblies of God church he pastored began to care for those that were sleeping under a pier. In 1999, after being challenged by the story of the Good Samaritan who put his hand in his own pocket to pay for the wellbeing of the battered man on the roadside, Pastor Pete and three members of the congregation put their hands in their own pockets to buy the first property for the poor and marginalised. These efforts to help the poor and marginalised have developed into the Christian social enterprise called Green Pastures (www.greenpastures.co.uk). Pastor Pete is the co-founder and director of Green Pastures which is now in the four countries of the UK and has housed and supported thousands of people by the Almighty's power. He and his wife Linda have six children together and nineteen grandchildren.

Working together to house the homeless.

Green Pastures is a Christian social enterprise that was founded in 1999, by Pastor Pete Cunningham, Vicki Woodley and Andrew Cunningham. We've been chasing one ambitious goal ever since: ending homelessness. We started from a local church in Southport, offering a home to those in need on our doorstep. Since then we have empowered churches and Christian organisations nationwide to house more than 10,000 people - changing lives and transforming hearts.

While the homelessness crisis is huge, we're optimistic. We have seen amazing changes in people simply by giving them a key to their own home and offering compassionate support.

We make progress every day thanks to the help of local Partners and income from our Investors. If we work together, we believe everyone can have a safe and secure home, and the support and care that they need.

Find out more about our ministy, and how you can get involved at **greenpastures.co.uk.**

An ethical investment that changes a life.

Imagine lending some of your money to help give a home and support to people who are homeless, whilst you earn a return.

That's the smart but simple idea behind investing with Green Pastures: We put your money to good work buying properties that are used by our local charity partners to house the homeless and change lives.

You can invest from £1000, earn up to 5% annually, and help transform lives. Find out more and start investing with Green Pastures by visiting our website: **greenpastures.co.uk/invest**.

Partnering with you to house the homeless.

If you're interested in making a difference in the lives of those facing homelessness, Green Pastures could partner with you in housing the homeless in your area.

We work in partnership with local Christian ministries across the UK to offer a home and support to the homeless: We buy the property, provide all the tools needed to offer a home to people in need, and work together with our Partners for the long term to help change lives.

Read more about how our partnership model works and make an enquiry to one of our team based in your area on our website: **greenpastures.co.uk/housing**.

Printed in Great Britain
by Amazon

28755012R00096